FOR ORGANS, PIANOS & ELECTRONIC KEYBOARDS

**E-Z PLAY TODAY**

**208**

EASY LISTENING FAVORITES

MW00528133

## CONTENTS

ISBN 0-7935-8240-7

HAL•LEONARD®
CORPORATION
7777 W. BLUEMOUND RD. P.O. BOX 13819 MILWAUKEE, WI 53213

E-Z PLAY ® TODAY Music Notation © 1975 HAL LEONARD CORPORATION

Visit Hal Leonard Online at
**www.halleonard.com**

# Alfie
## Theme from the Paramount Picture ALFIE

Registration 9
Rhythm: 8 Beat or Pops

Words by Hal David
Music by Burt Bacharach

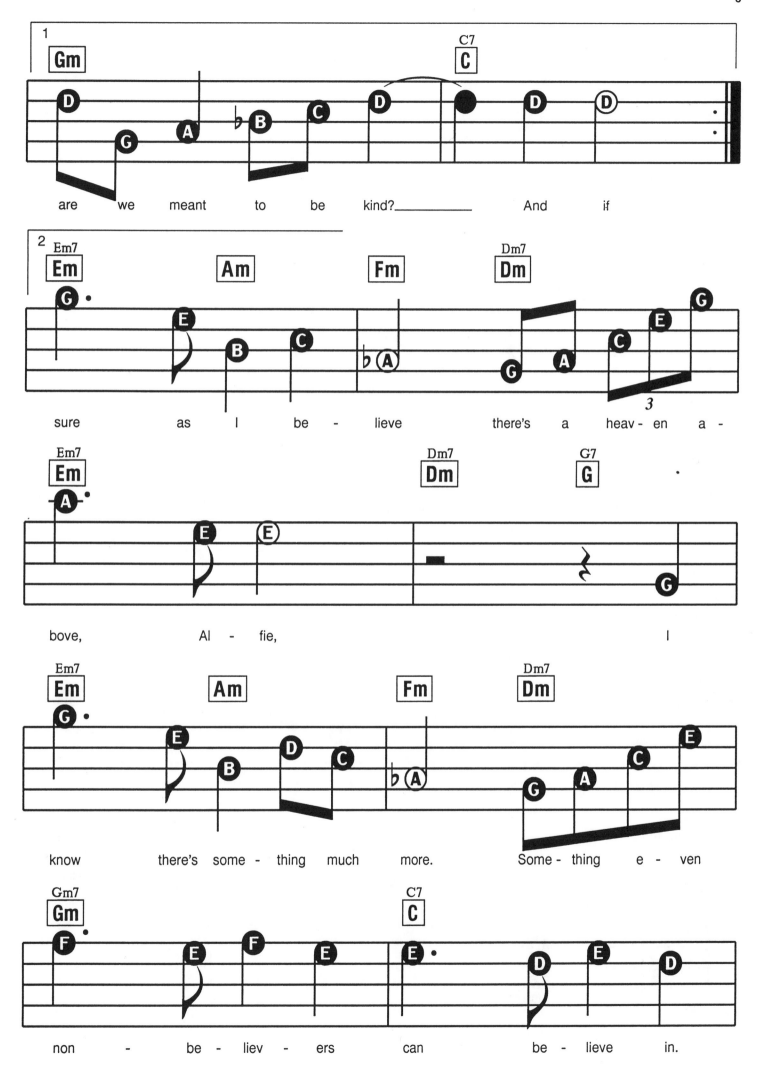

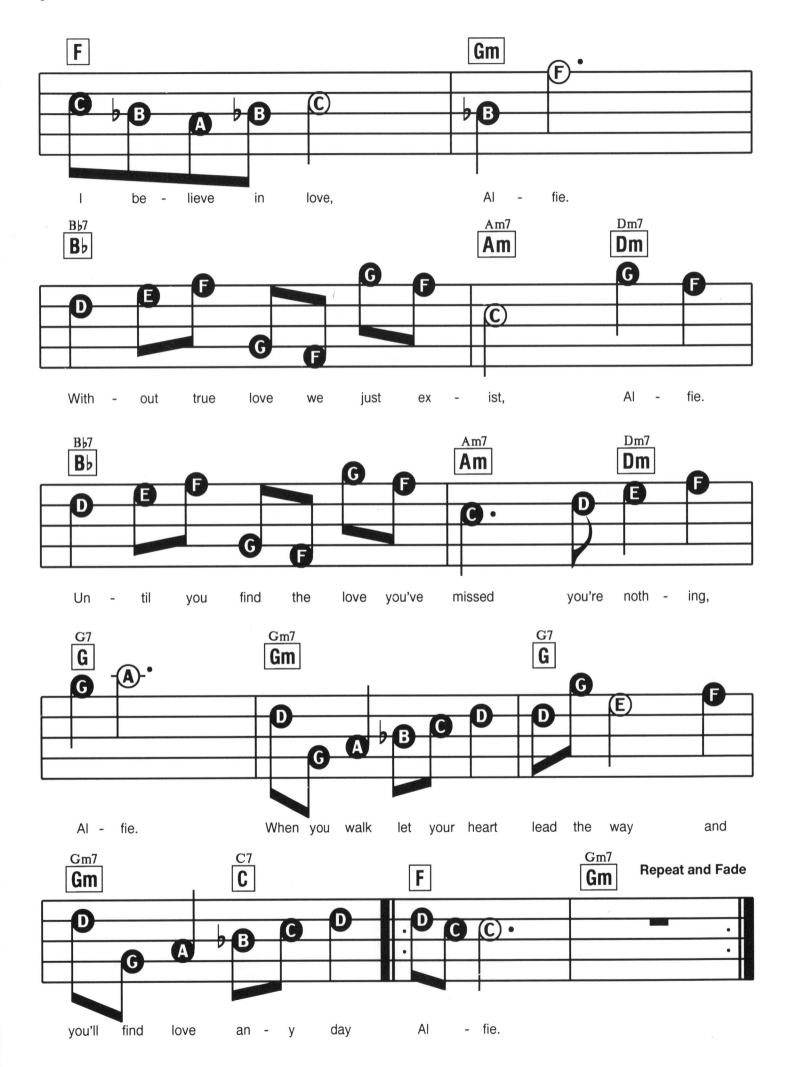

# And I Love You So

Registration 3
Rhythm: Pops or 8 Beat

Words and Music by
Don McLean

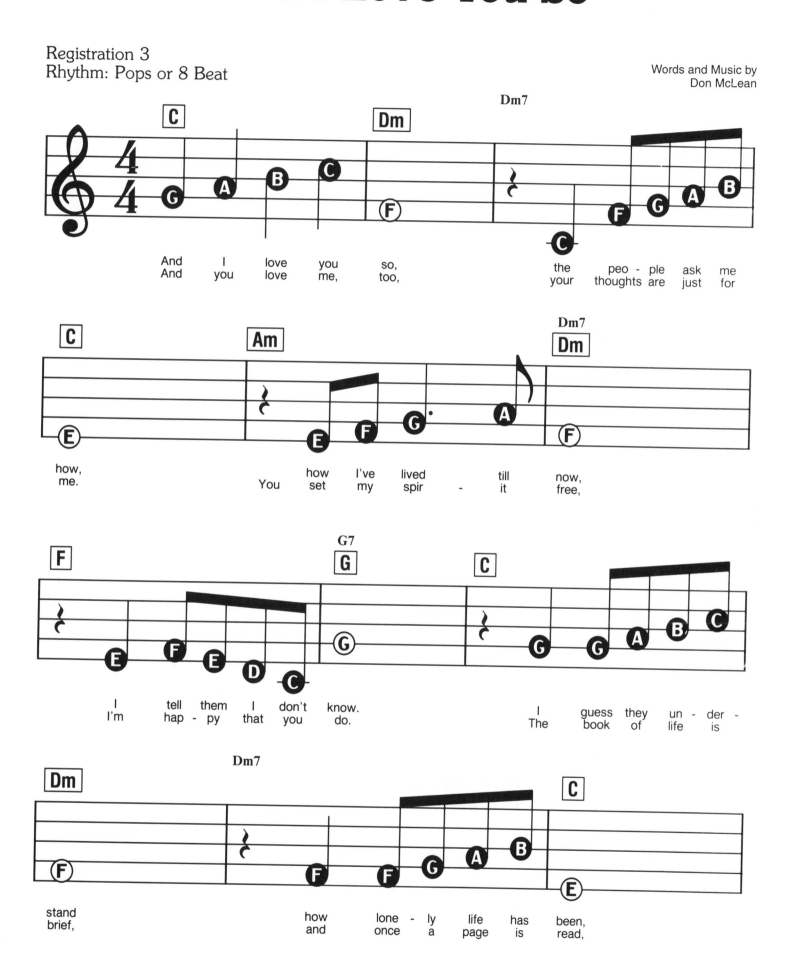

**MCA** music publishing

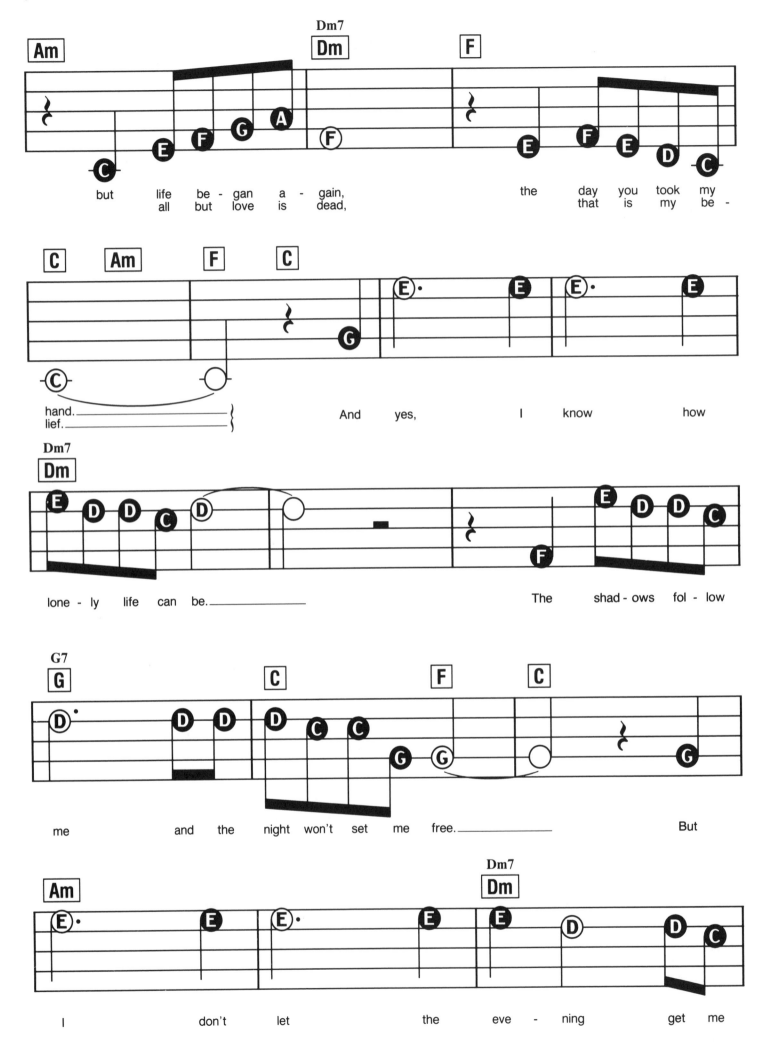

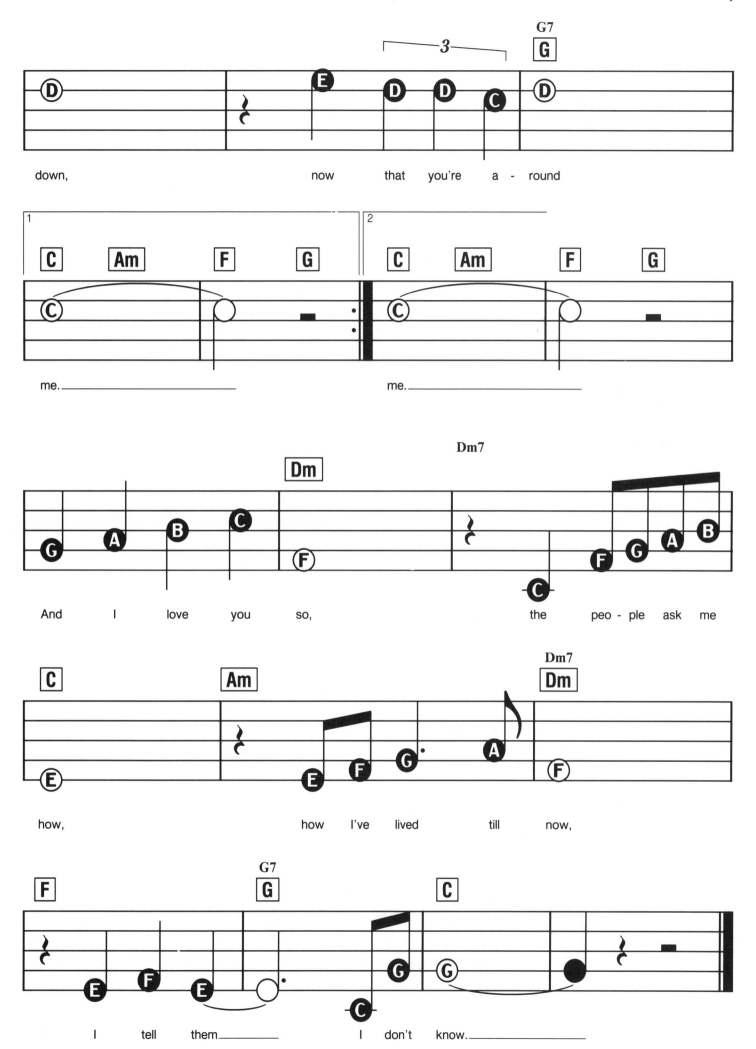

8

# Always on My Mind

Registration 10
Rhythm: Ballad or Slow Rock

Words and Music by Wayne Thompson,
Mark James and Johnny Christopher

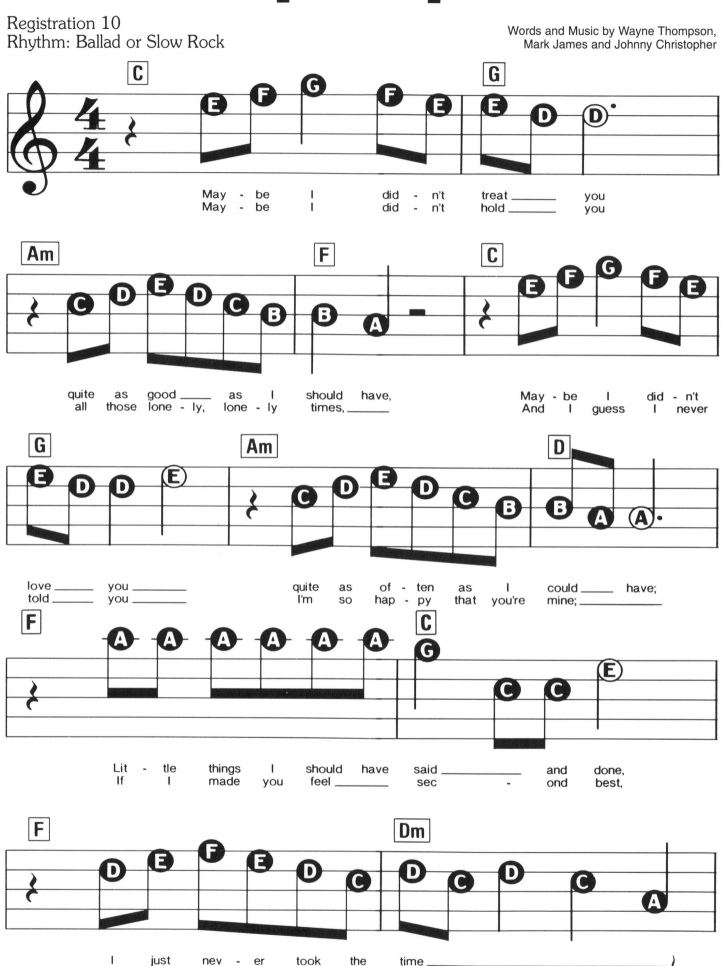

© 1971, 1979 SCREEN GEMS-EMI MUSIC INC. and BUDDE SONGS INC.
All Rights Controlled and Administered by SCREEN GEMS-EMI MUSIC INC.
All Rights Reserved   International Copyright Secured   Used by Permission

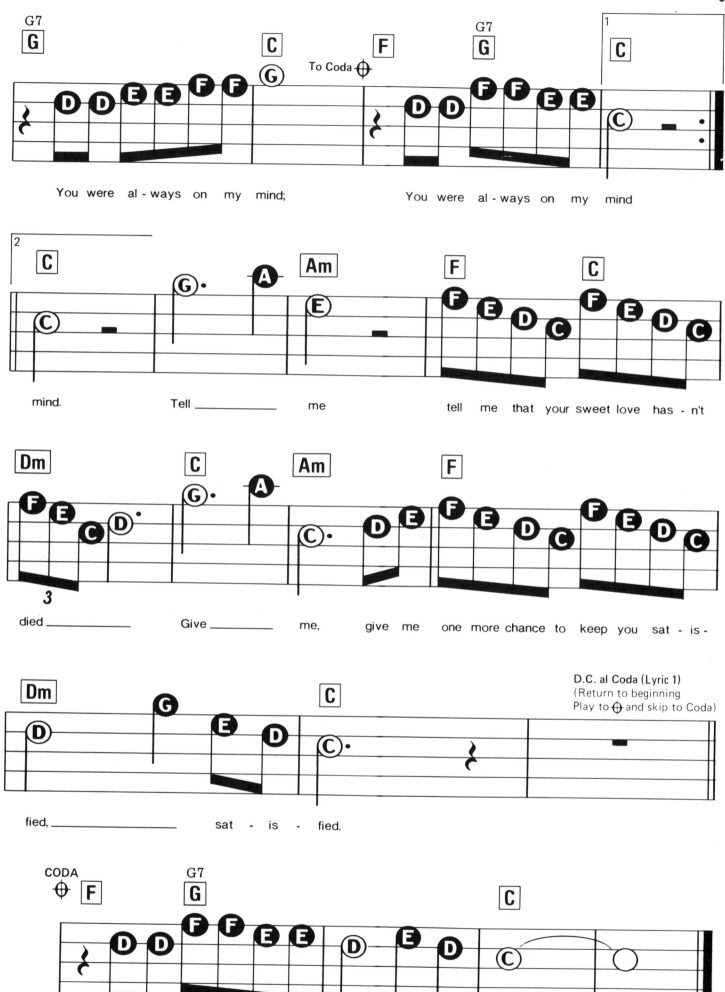

# Bless the Beasts and Children

Registration 3
Rhythm: Slow Rock or Ballad

Words and Music by Barry DeVorzon
and Perry Botkin, Jr.

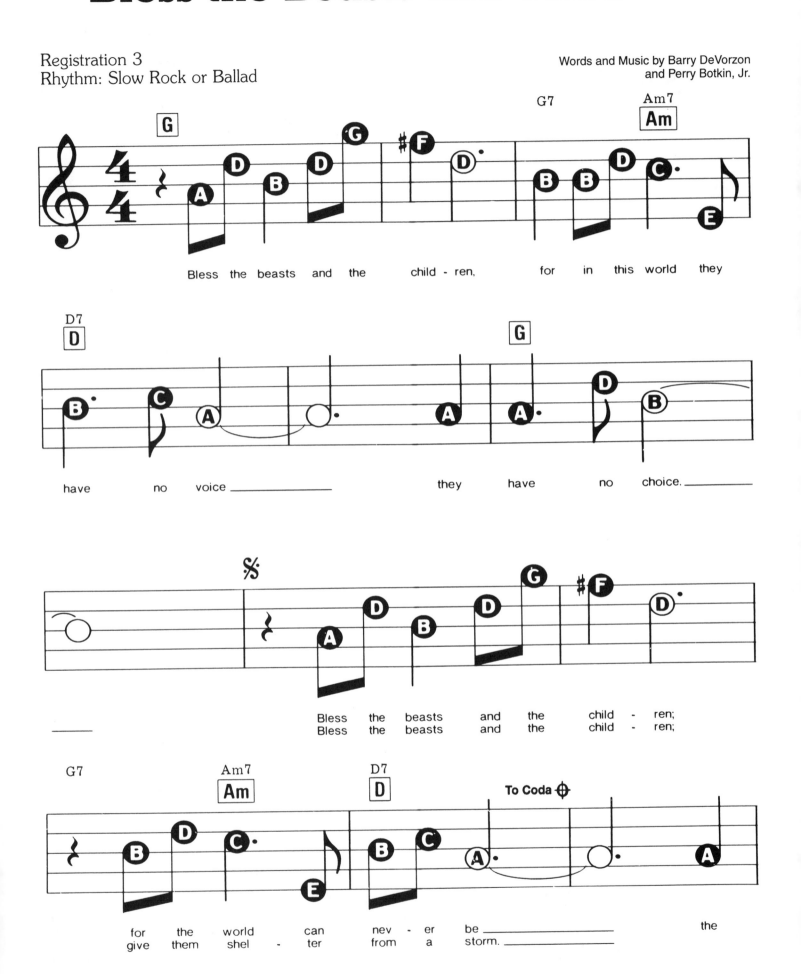

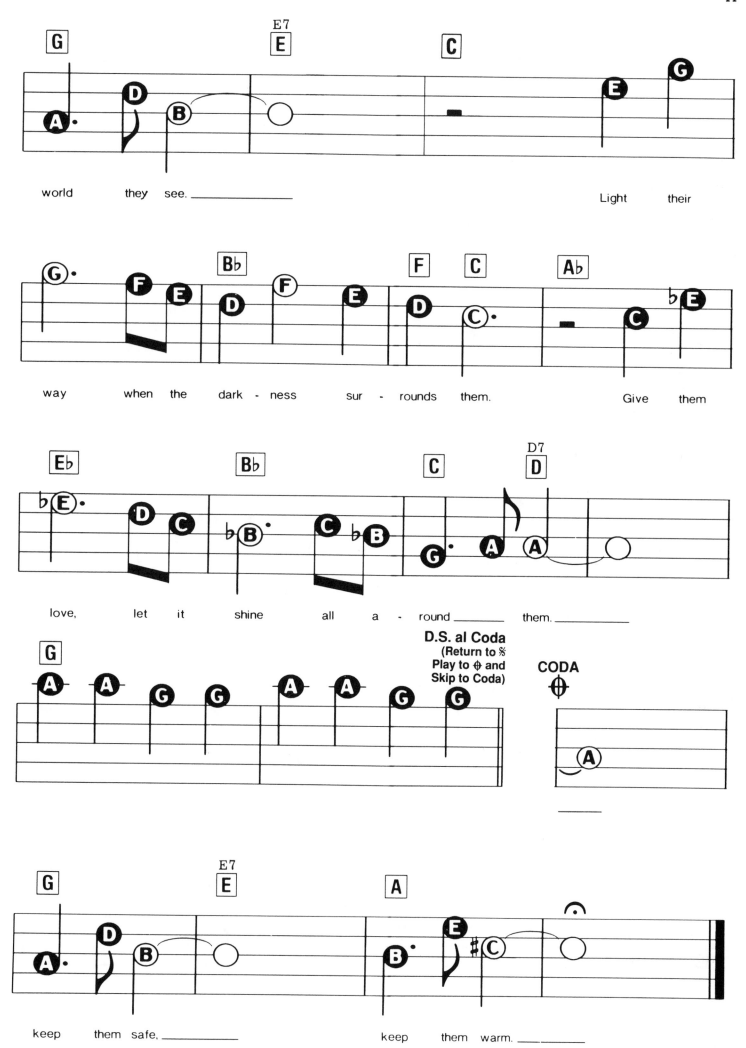

11

# Blue on Blue

Registration 4
Rhythm: Swing or Fox-Trot

Lyric by Hal David
Music by Burt Bacharach

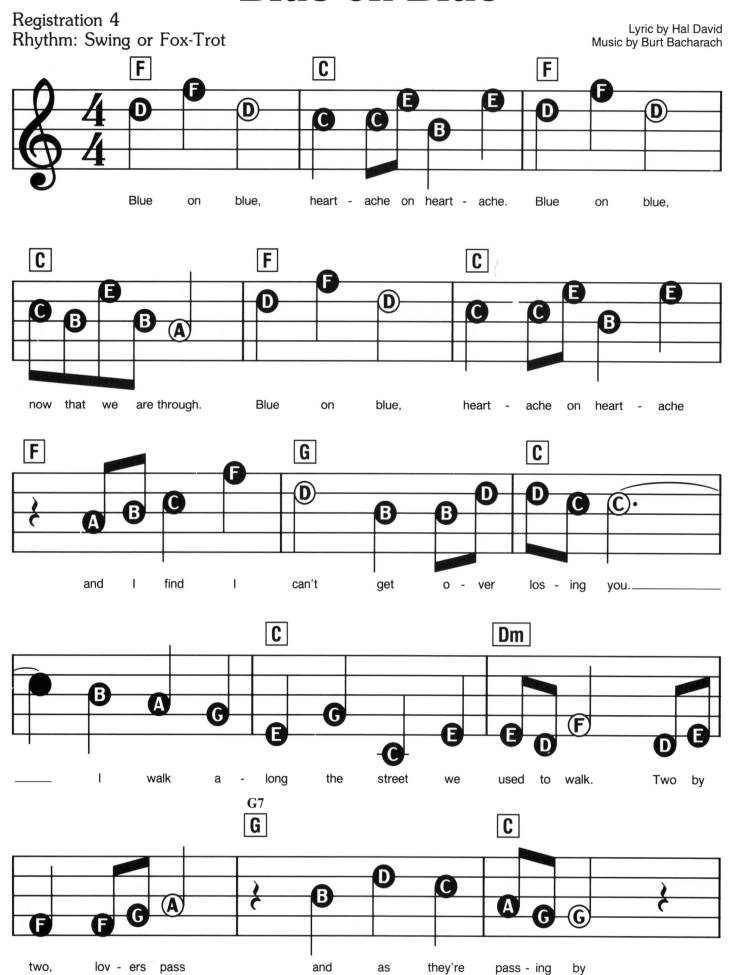

13

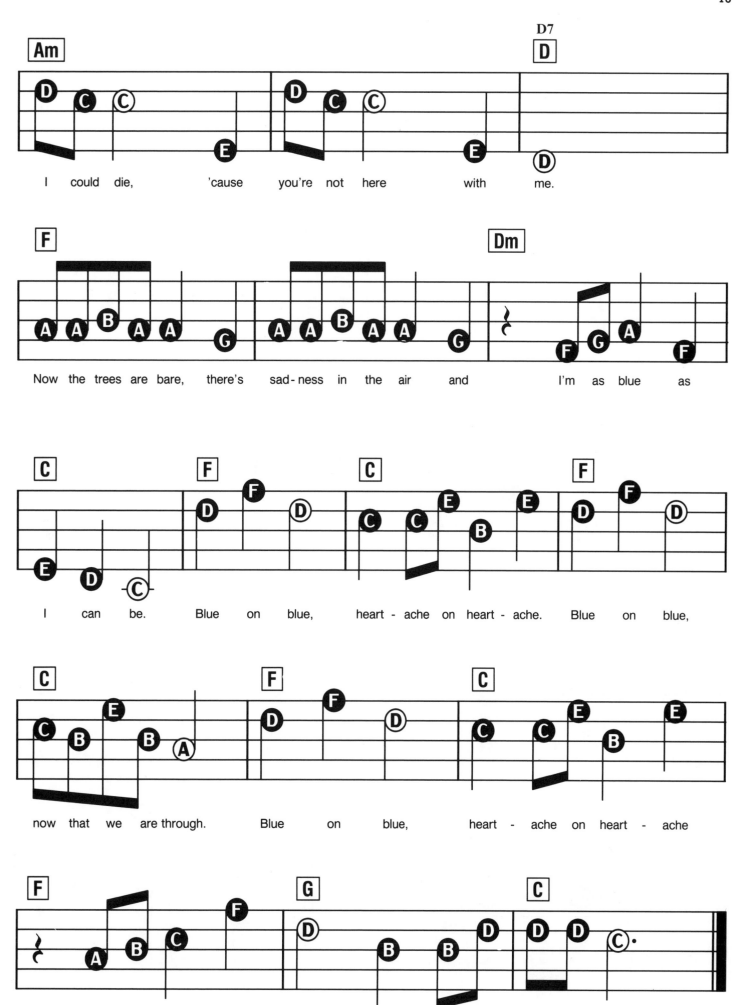

# Born Free
### from the Columbia Pictures' Release BORN FREE

Registration 4
Rhythm: Ballad

Words by Don Black
Music by John Barry

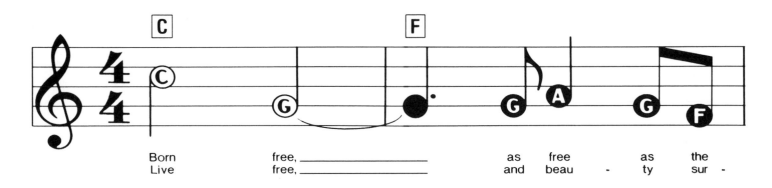

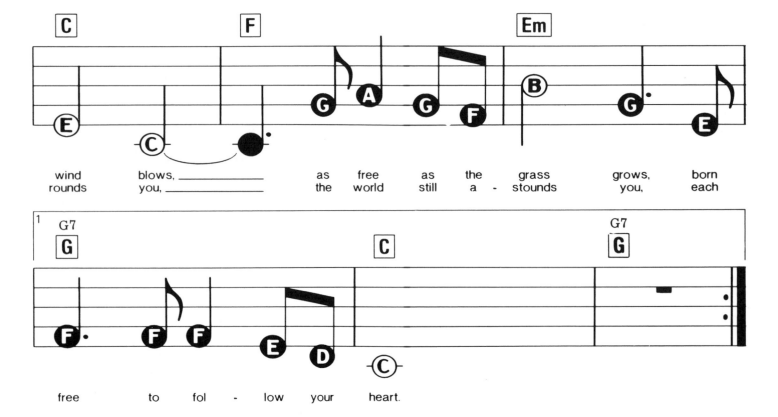

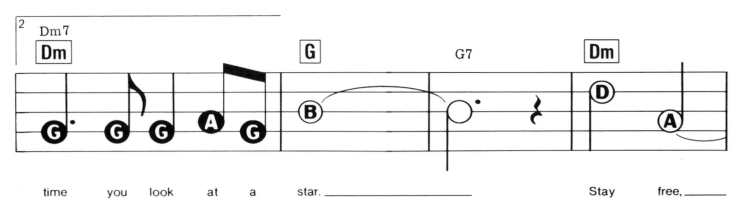

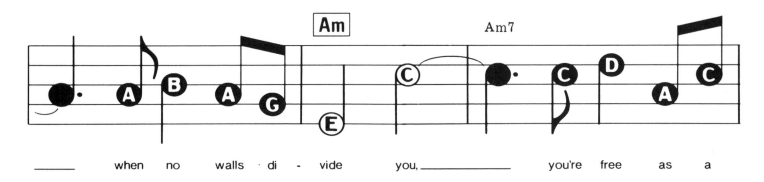

when no walls di - vide you, \_\_\_\_ you're free as a

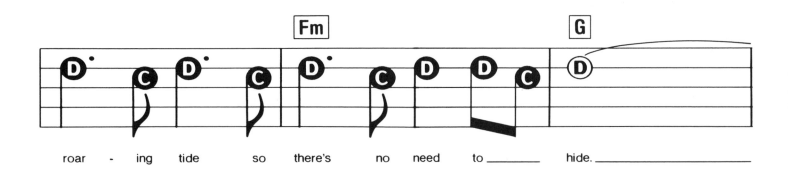

roar - ing tide so there's no need to \_\_\_\_ hide. \_\_\_\_

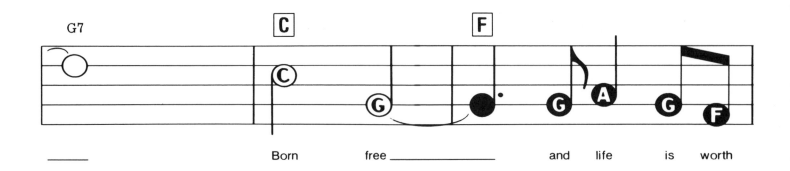

Born free \_\_\_\_ and life is worth

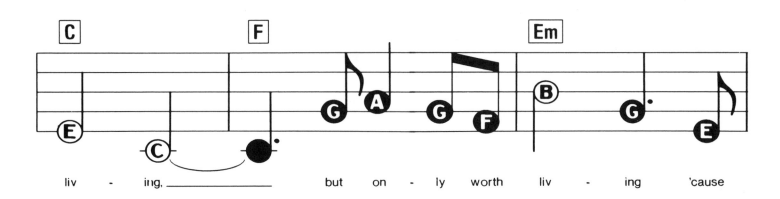

liv - ing, \_\_\_\_ but on - ly worth liv - ing 'cause

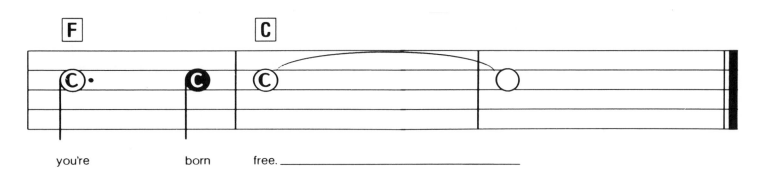

you're born free. \_\_\_\_

# Cherish

Registration 3
Rhythm: Rock or Disco

Words and Music by
Terry Kirkman

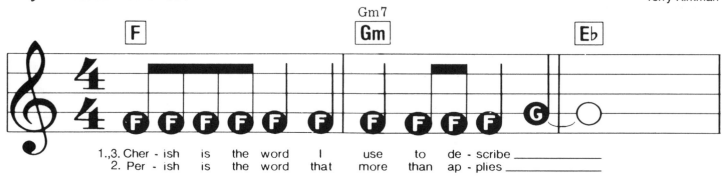

1.,3. Cher - ish is the word I use to de - scribe _____
2. Per - ish is the word that more than ap - plies _____

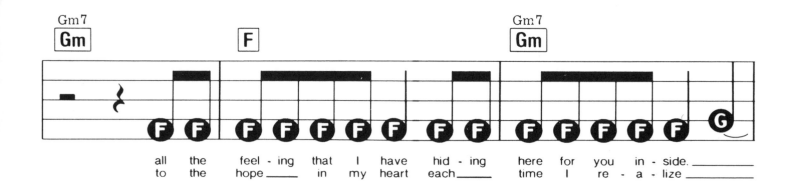

all the feel - ing that I have hid - ing here for you in - side. _____
to the hope _____ in my heart each _____ time I re - a - lize _____

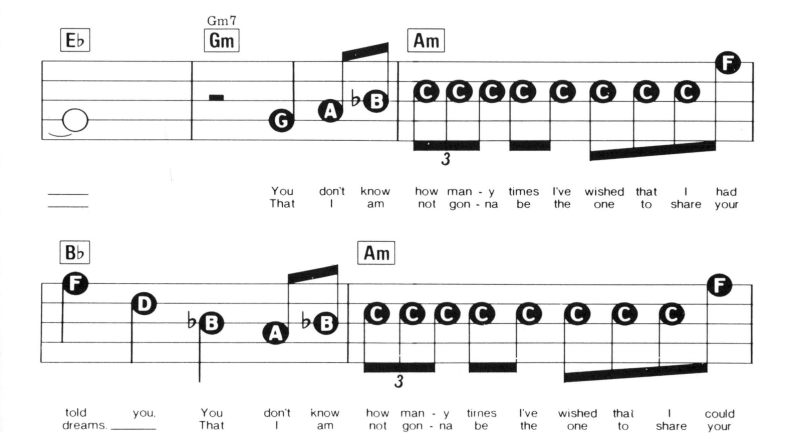

_____ You don't know how man - y times I've wished that I had
That I am not gon - na be the one to share your

told you. You don't know how man - y times I've wished that I could
dreams. _____ That I am not gon - na be the one to share your

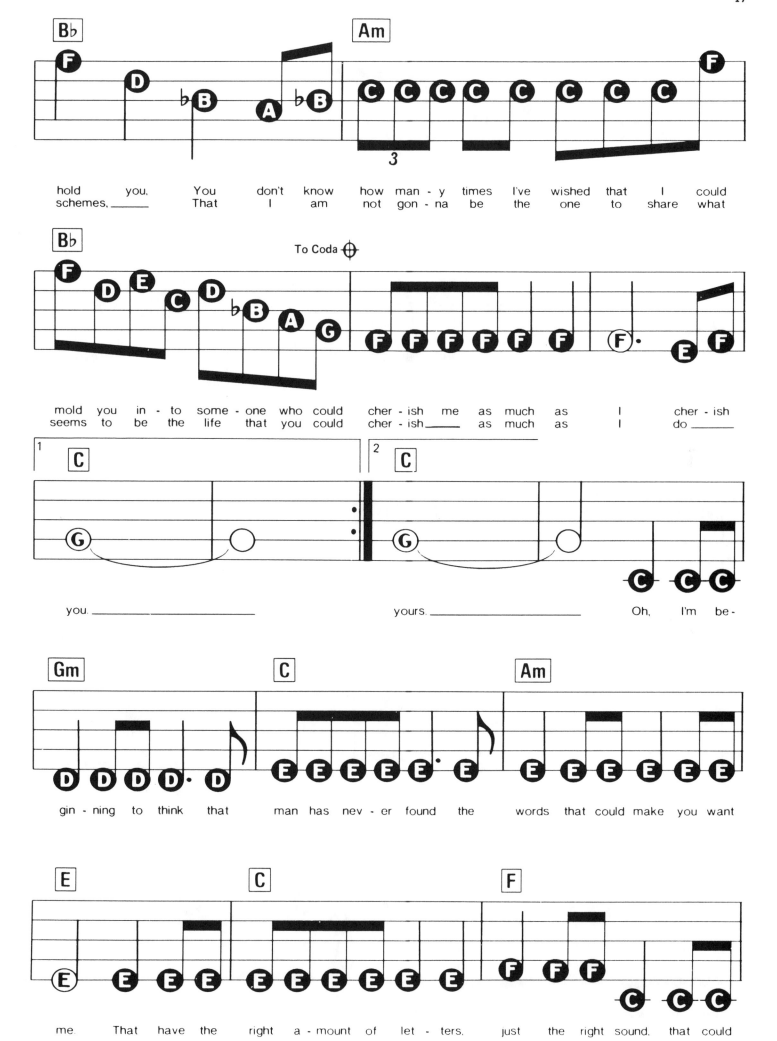

18

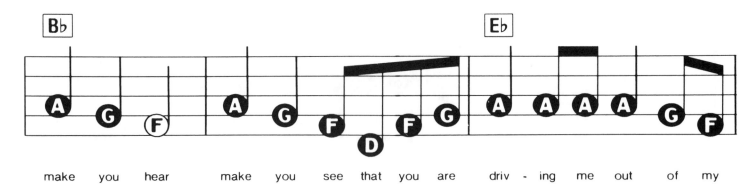

make you hear make you see that you are driv - ing me out of my

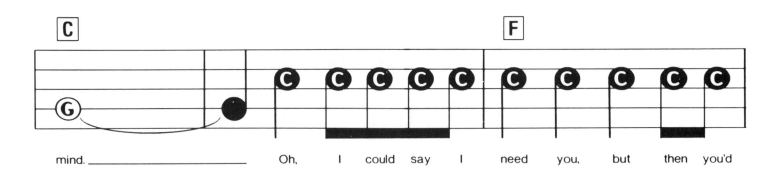

mind. _____ Oh, I could say I need you, but then you'd

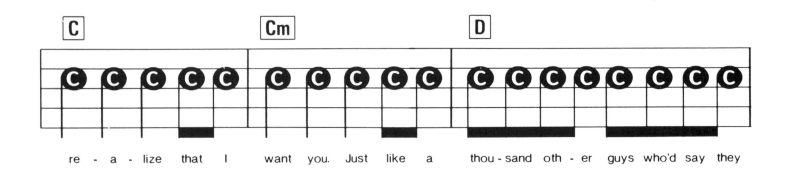

re - a - lize that I want you. Just like a thou - sand oth - er guys who'd say they

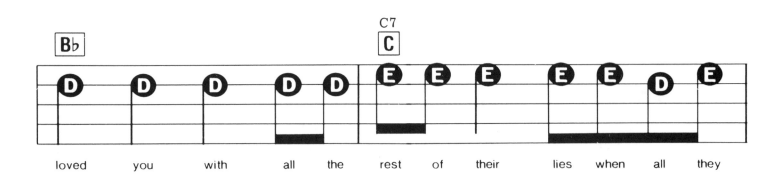

loved you with all the rest of their lies when all they

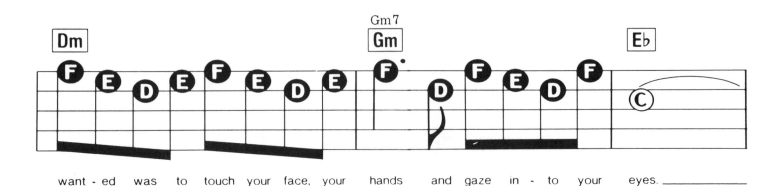

want - ed was to touch your face, your hands and gaze in - to your eyes. _____

19

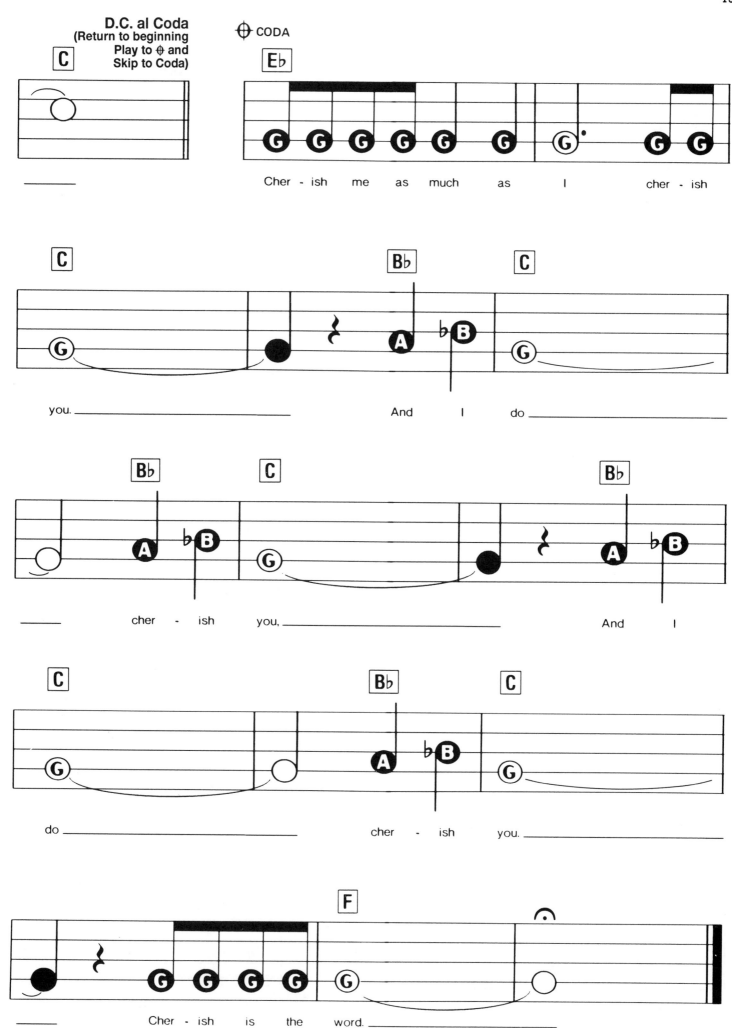

# Come Saturday Morning
## (Saturday Morning)
### from the Paramount Picture THE STERILE CUCKOO

Registration 1
Rhythm: Waltz

Words by Dory Previn
Music by Fred Karlin

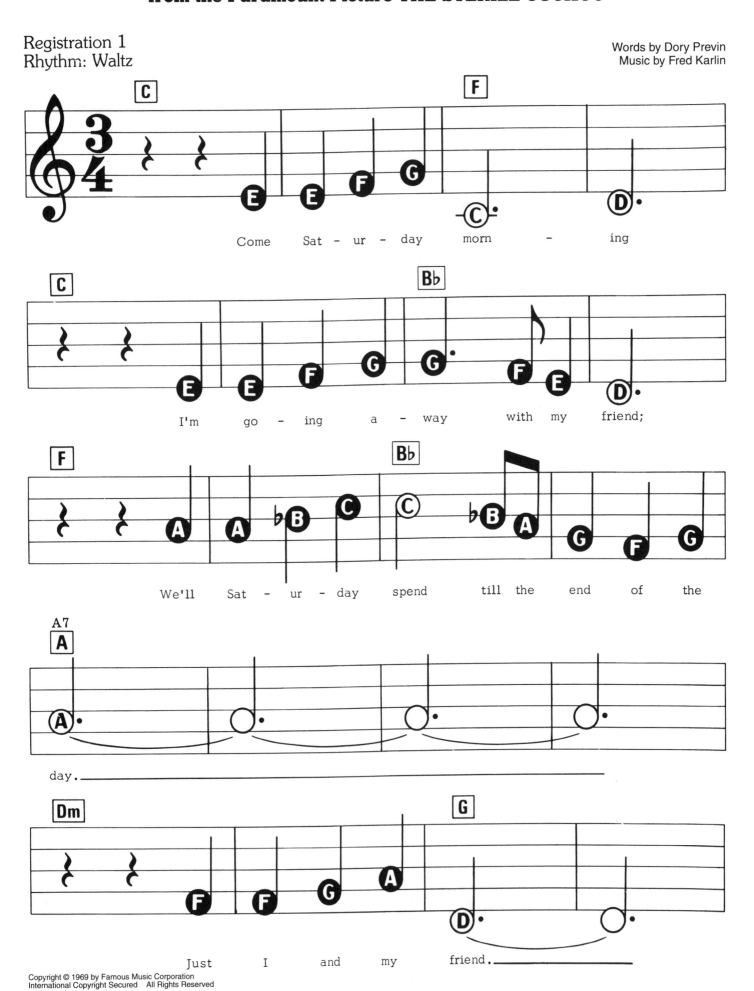

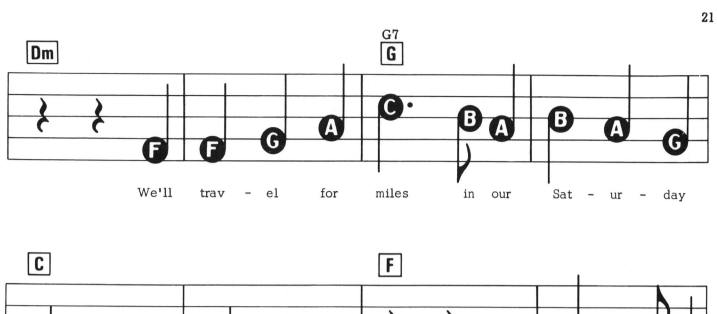

We'll trav - el for miles in our Sat - ur - day

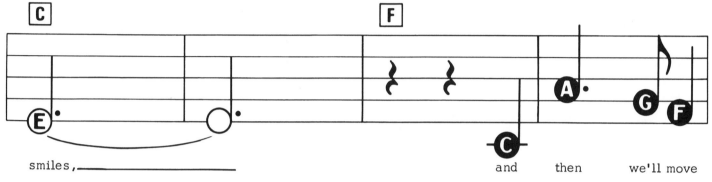

smiles,_____ and then we'll move

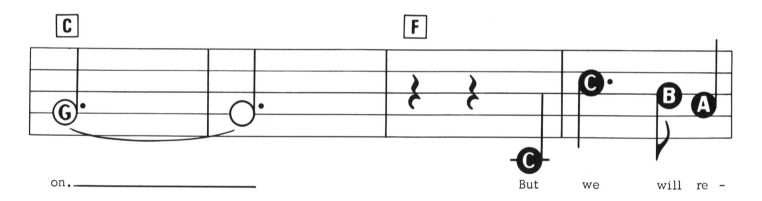

on._____ But we will re -

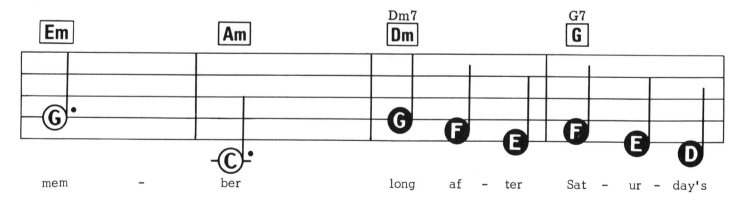

mem - ber long af - ter Sat - ur - day's

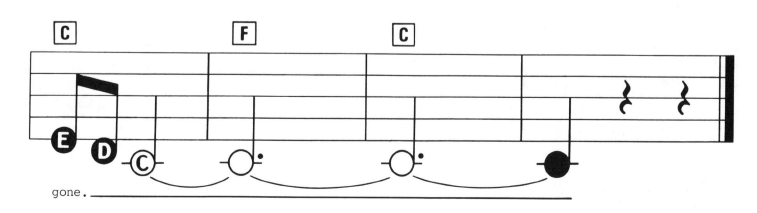

gone._____

# Do You Know Where You're Going To?

### Theme from MAHOGANY

Words by Gerry Goffin
Music by Mike Masser

Registration 5
Rhythm: Slow Rock or Ballad

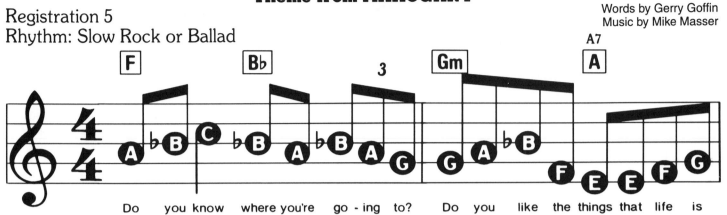

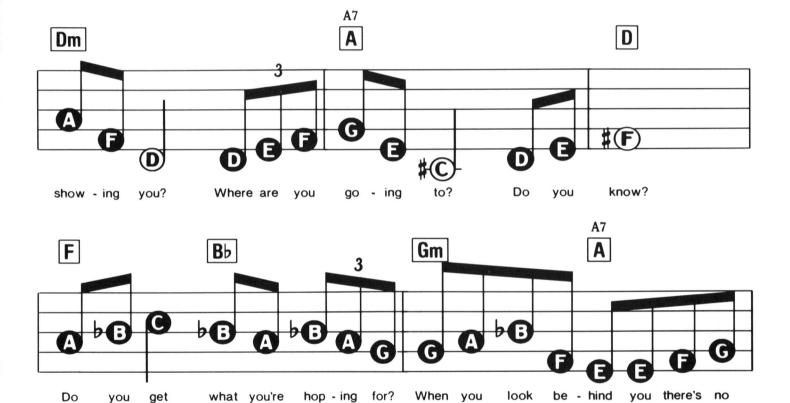

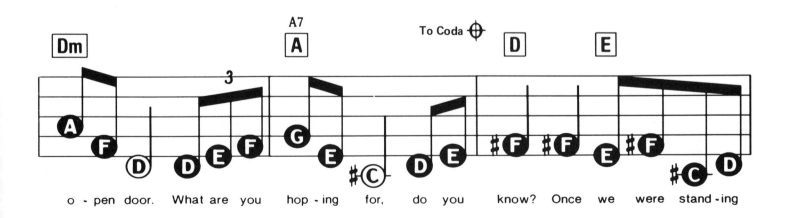

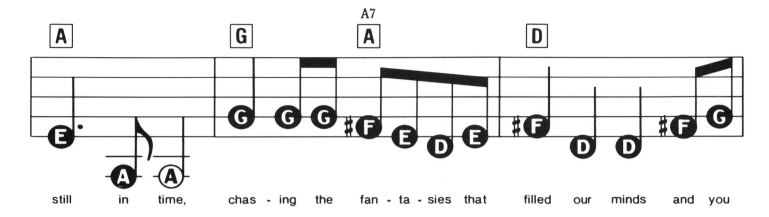

still in time, chas-ing the fan-ta-sies that filled our minds and you

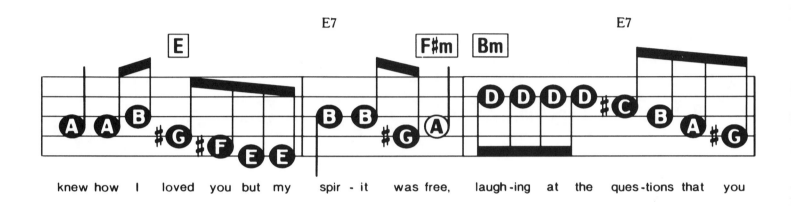

knew how I loved you but my spir-it was free, laugh-ing at the ques-tions that you

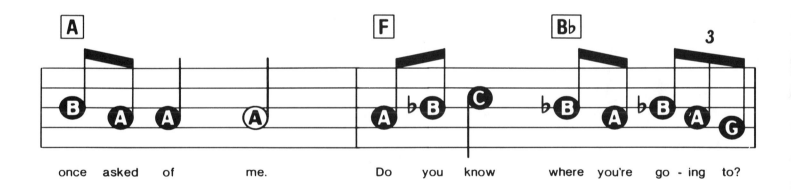

once asked of me. Do you know where you're go-ing to?

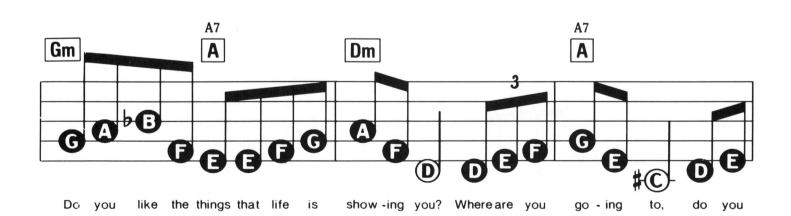

Do you like the things that life is show-ing you? Where are you go-ing to, do you

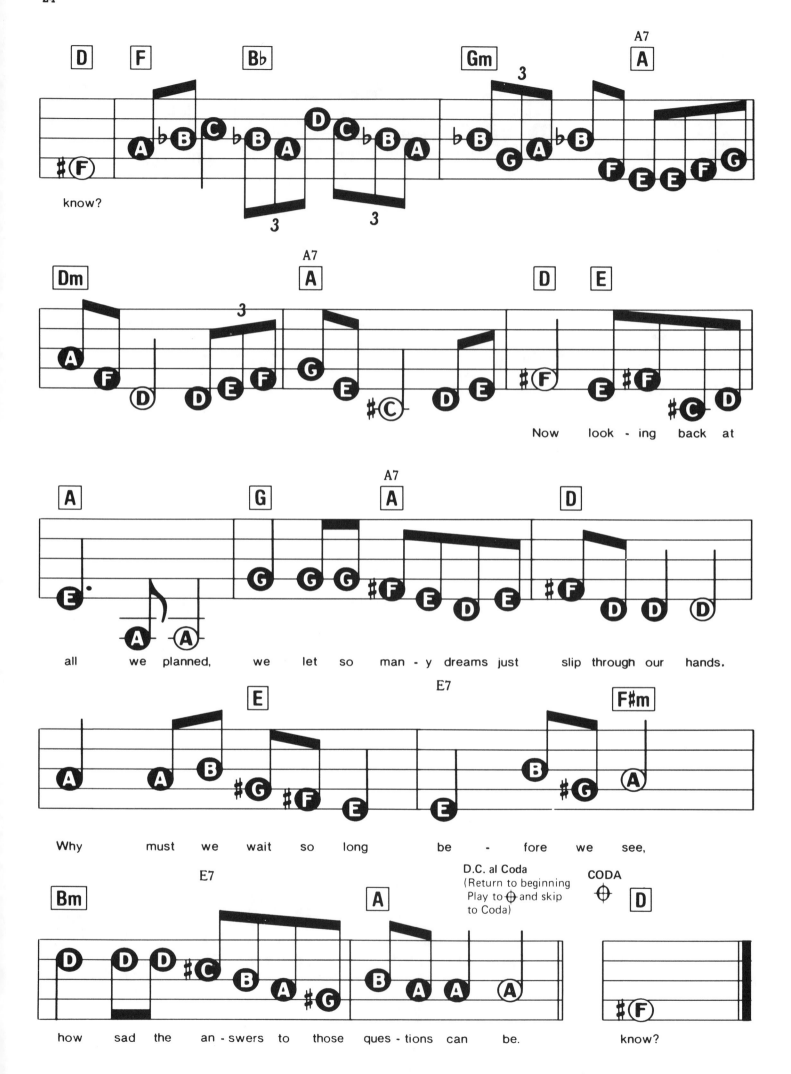

# One Less Bell to Answer

Registration 8
Rhythm: Swing Shuffle, or Fox Trot

Lyric by Hal David
Music by Burt Bacharach

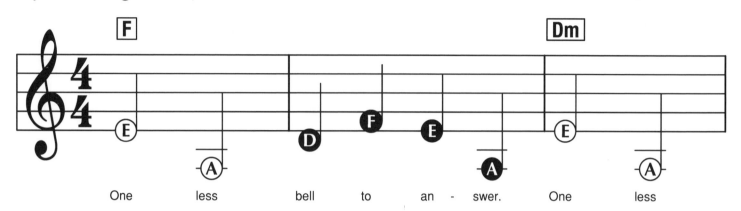

One     less     bell   to   an  -  swer.       One     less

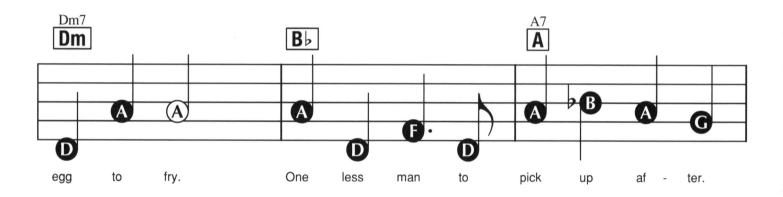

egg    to   fry.      One   less  man   to    pick   up   af - ter.

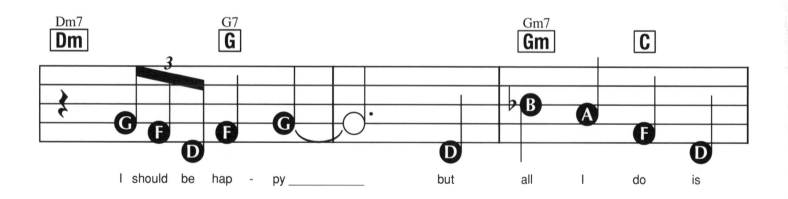

I   should  be  hap - py _____     but    all   I    do   is

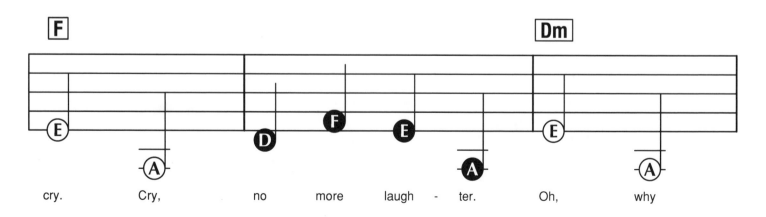

cry.      Cry,     no    more   laugh - ter.      Oh,      why

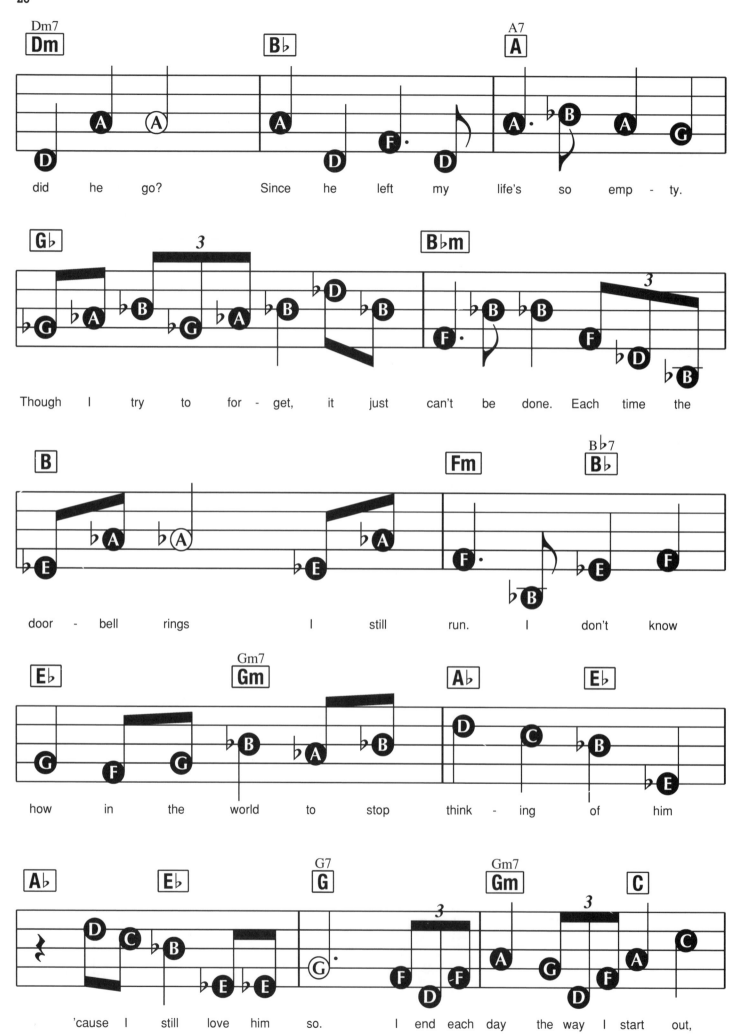

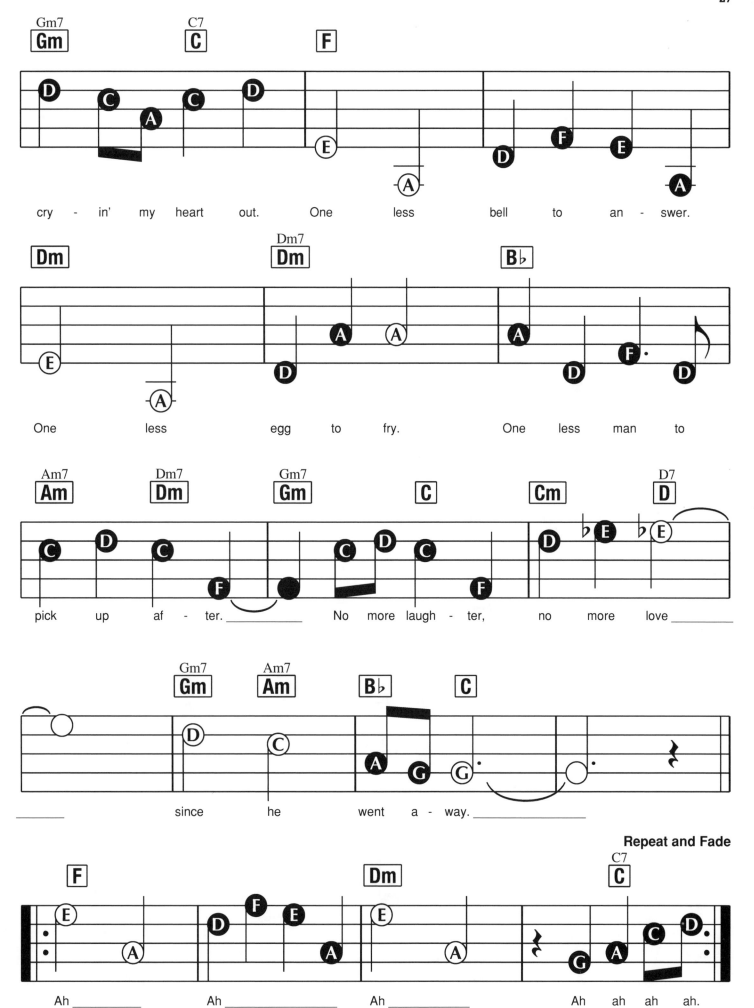

cry - in' my heart out. One less bell to an - swer.

One less egg to fry. One less man to

pick up af - ter. _____ No more laugh - ter, no more love _____

_____ since he went a - way. _____

**Repeat and Fade**

Ah _____ Ah _____ Ah _____ Ah ah ah ah.

# I Write the Songs

Registration 7
Rhythm: Rock or 8 Beat

Words and Music by
Bruce Johnston

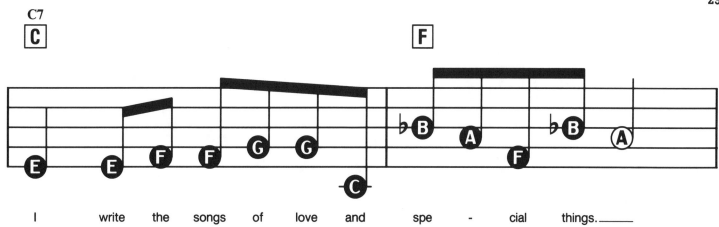

I write the songs of love and spe - cial things. _____

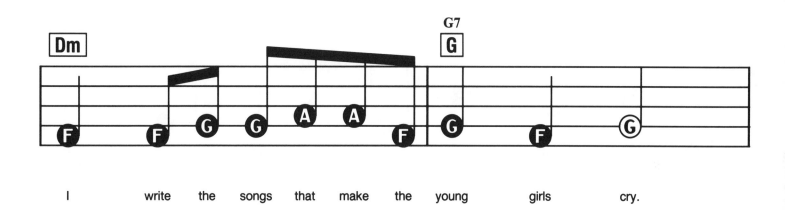

I write the songs that make the young girls cry.

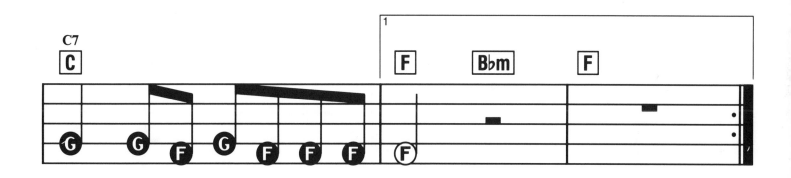

I write the songs, I write the songs.

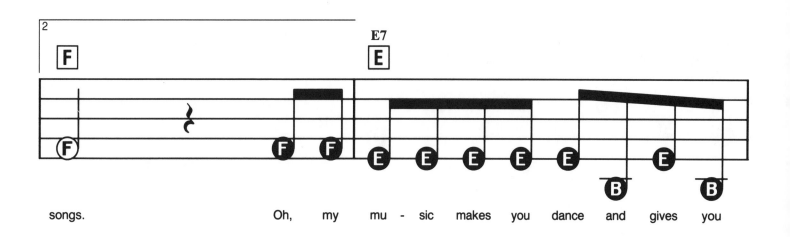

songs. Oh, my mu - sic makes you dance and gives you

30

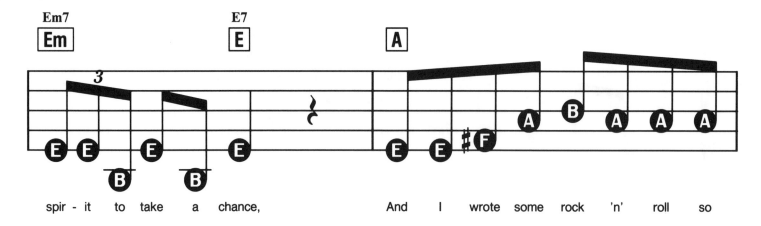

spir - it    to    take    a    chance,    And    I    wrote    some    rock    'n'    roll    so

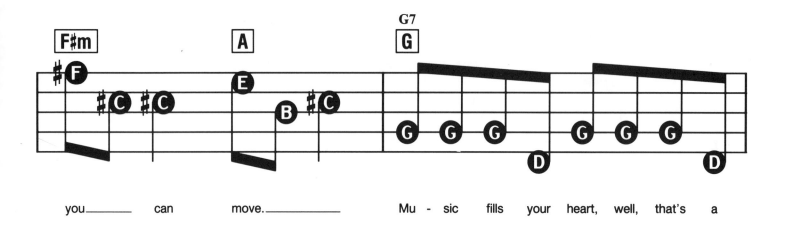

you____ can    move.____    Mu - sic    fills    your    heart,    well,    that's    a

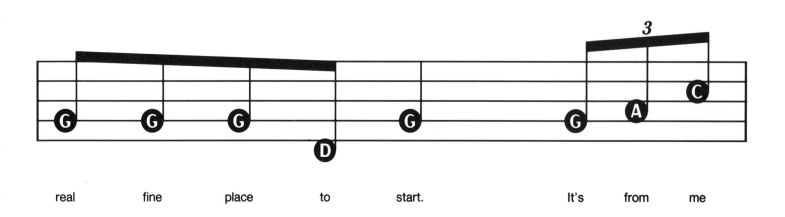

real    fine    place    to    start.    It's    from    me

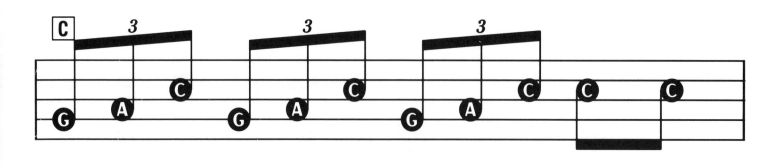

it's    for    you,    it's    from    you,    it's    for    me,    it's    a

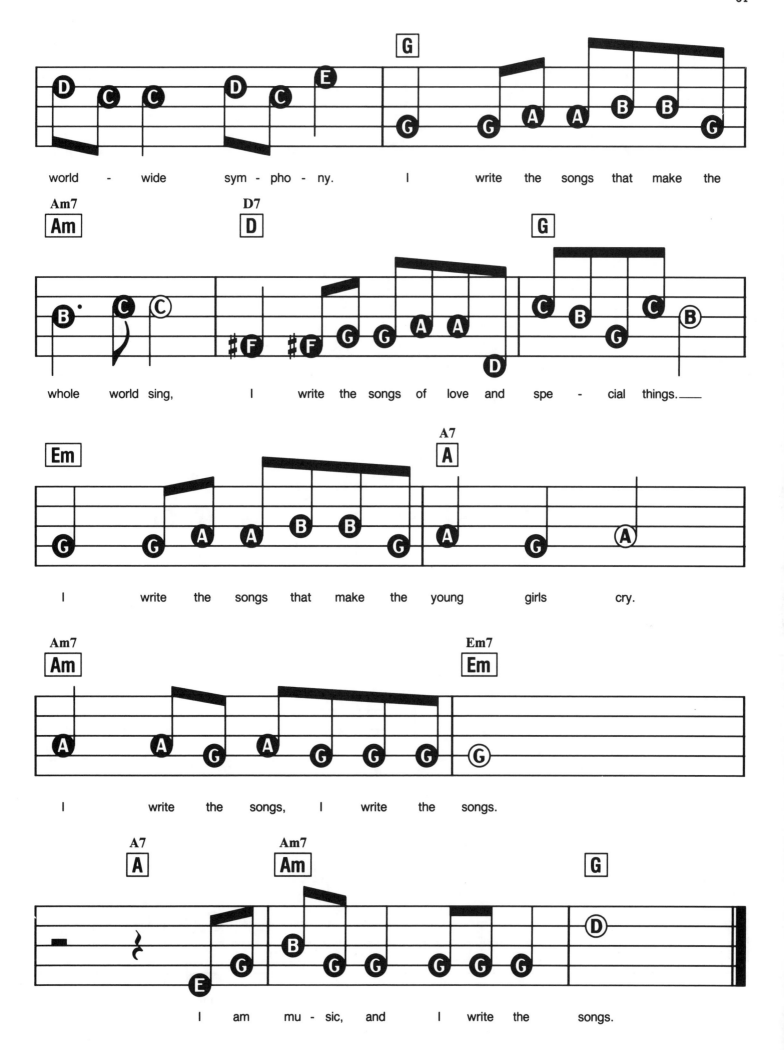

# If

Registration 2
Rhythm: Slow Rock or Ballad

Words and Music by
David Gates

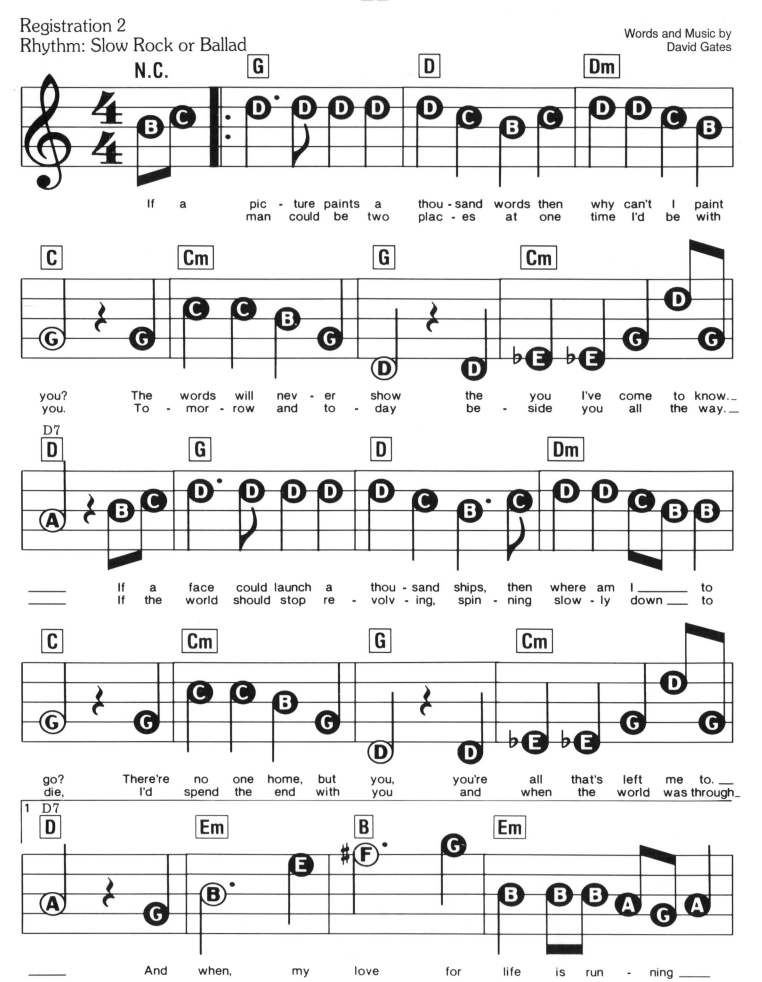

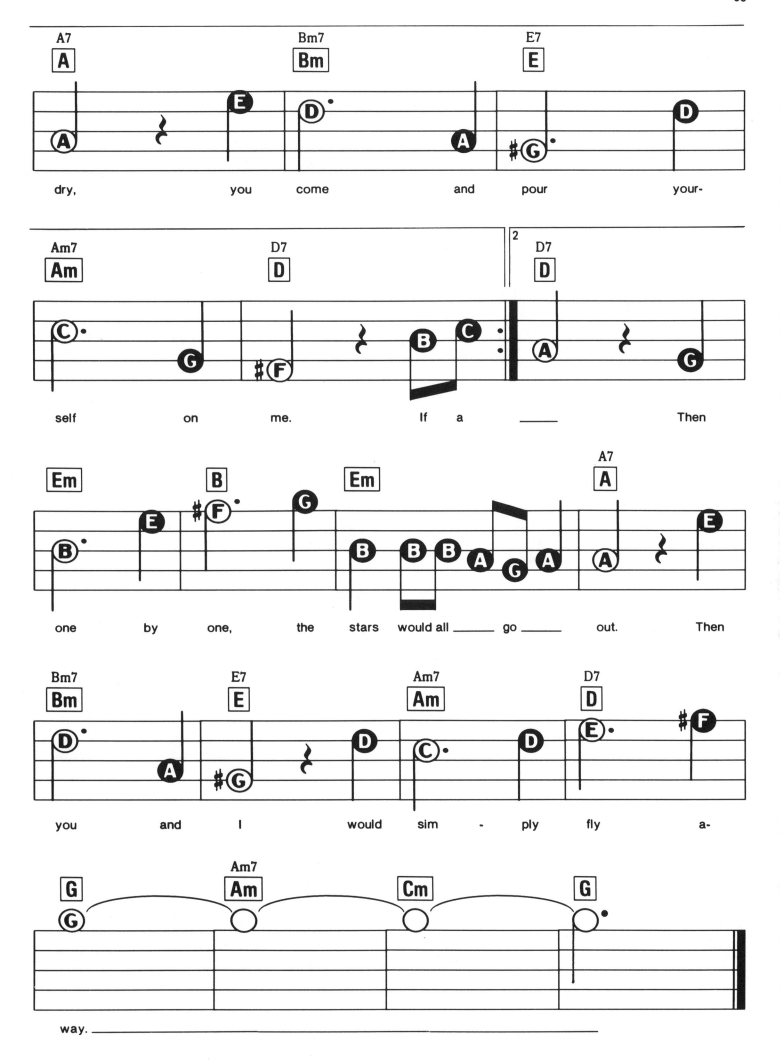

# Lollipops and Roses

Registration 2
Rhythm: Waltz

Words and Music by
Tony Velona

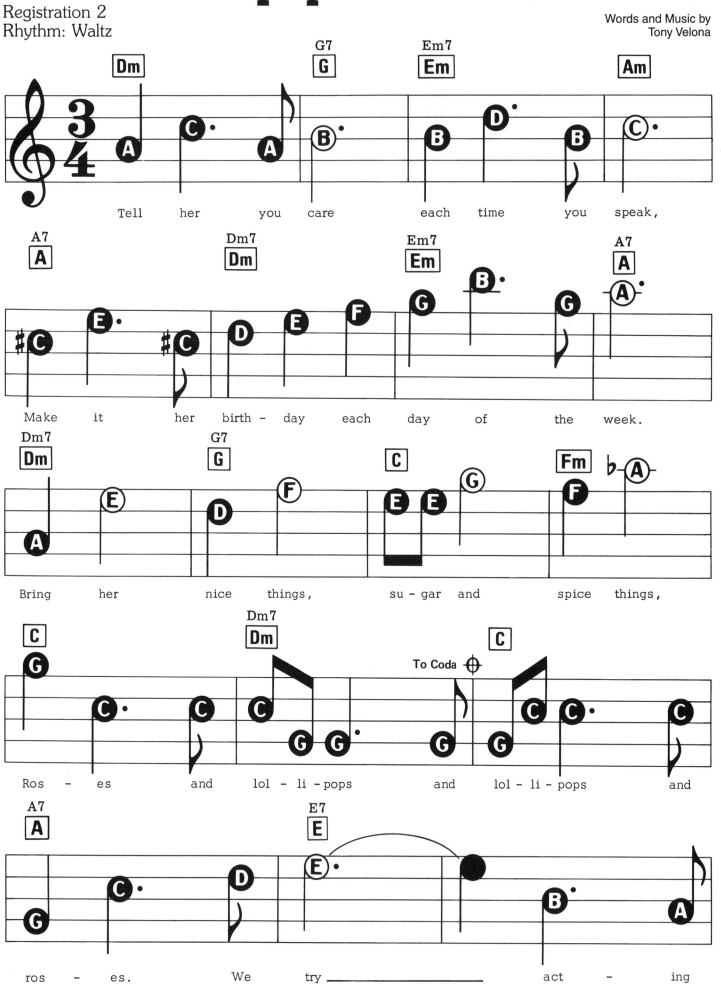

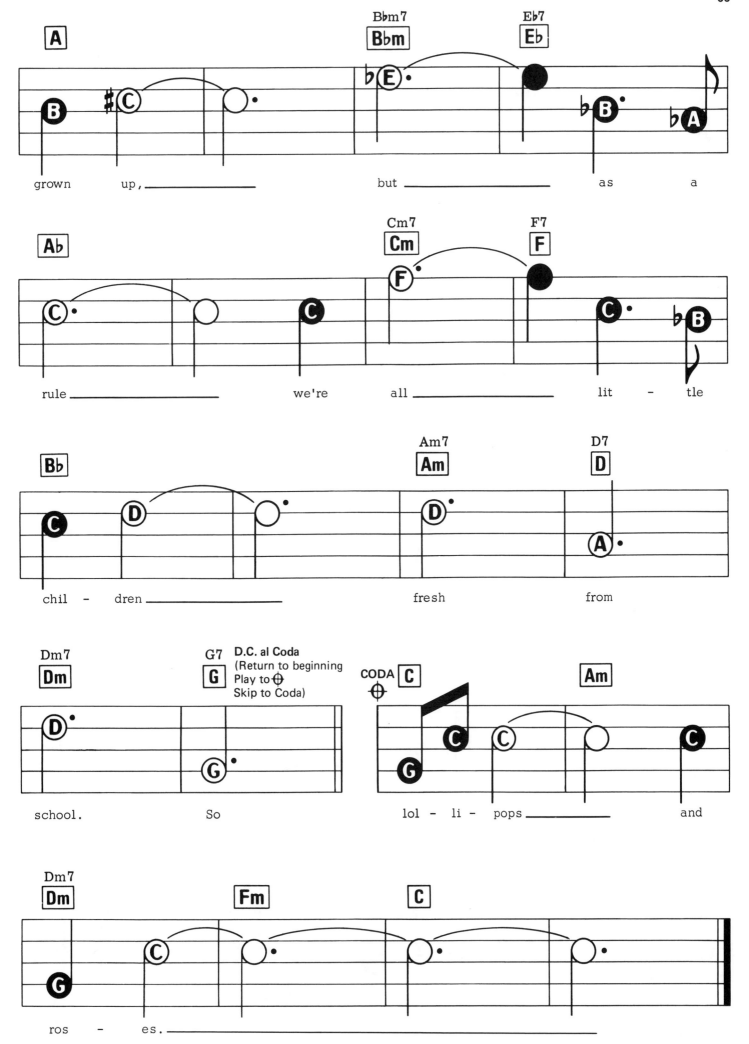

# The Look of Love
**from CASINO ROYALE**

Registration 4
Rhythm: Bossa Nova

Words by Hal David
Music by Burt Bacharach

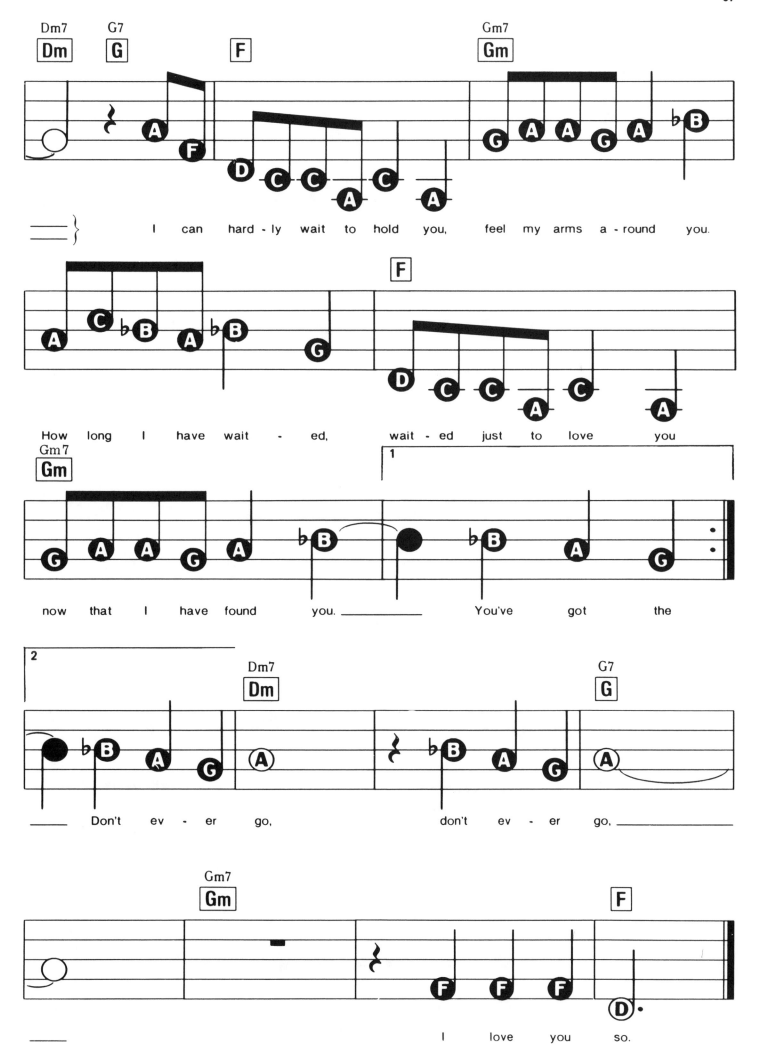

# Memories

Registration 2
Rhythm: Rock

Words and Music by Billy Strange
and Scott Davis

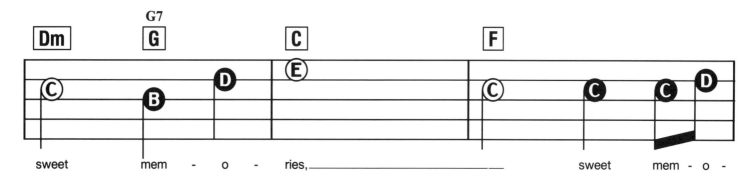

sweet mem - o - ries,_____ sweet mem - o -

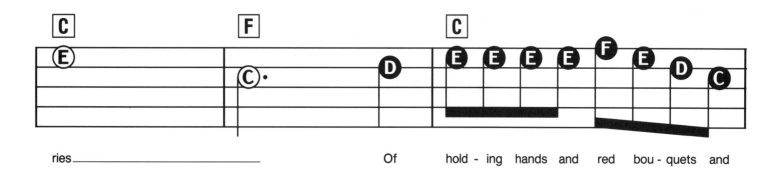

ries_____ Of hold - ing hands and red bou - quets and

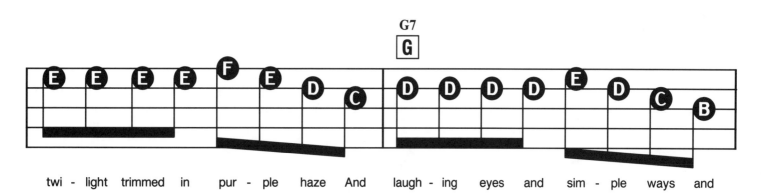

twi - light trimmed in pur - ple haze And laugh - ing eyes and sim - ple ways and

**D.C. al Coda**
(Return to beginning
Play to ⊕ and
skip to Coda)

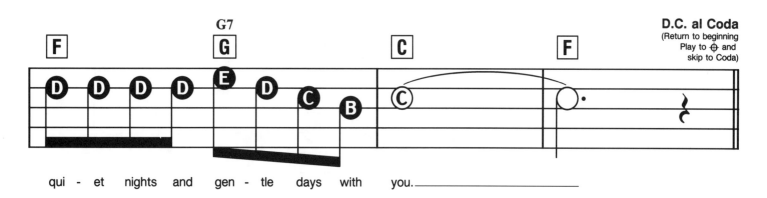

qui - et nights and gen - tle days with you._____

**CODA**

**Repeat and Fade**

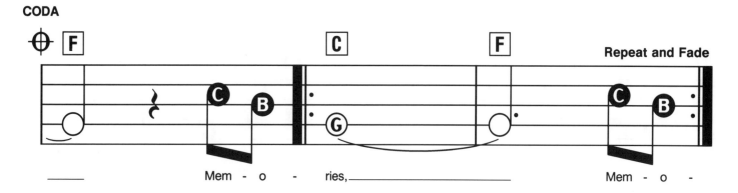

_____ Mem - o - ries,_____ Mem - o -

# Moon River

### from the Paramount Picture BREAKFAST AT TIFFANY'S

Registration 3
Rhythm: Waltz

Words by Johnny Mercer
Music by Henry Mancini

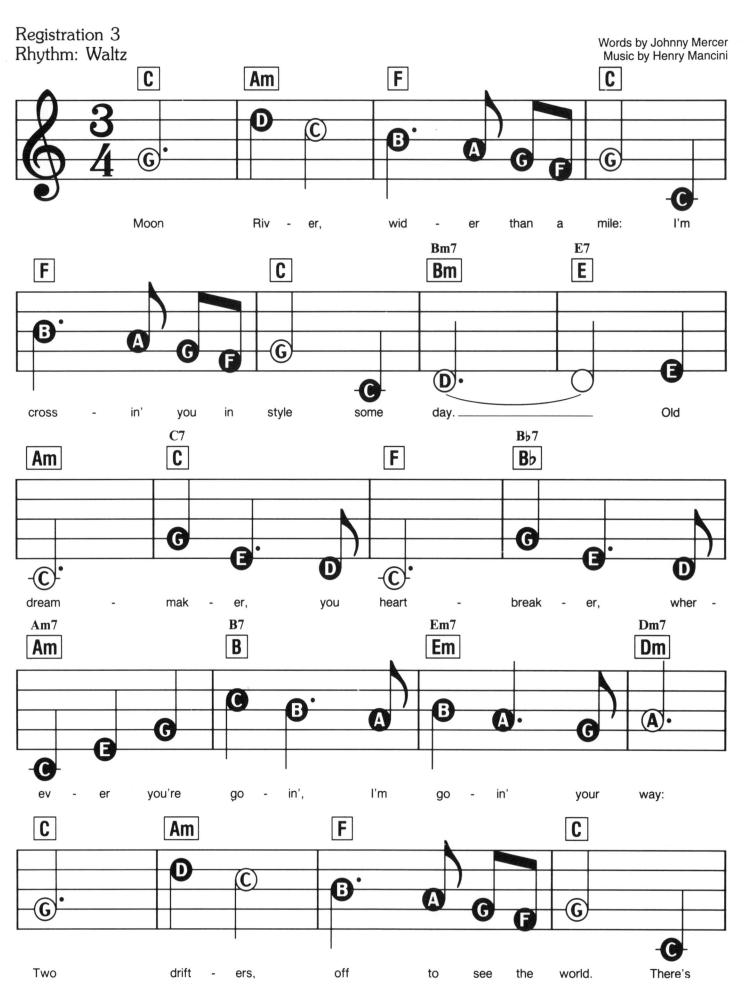

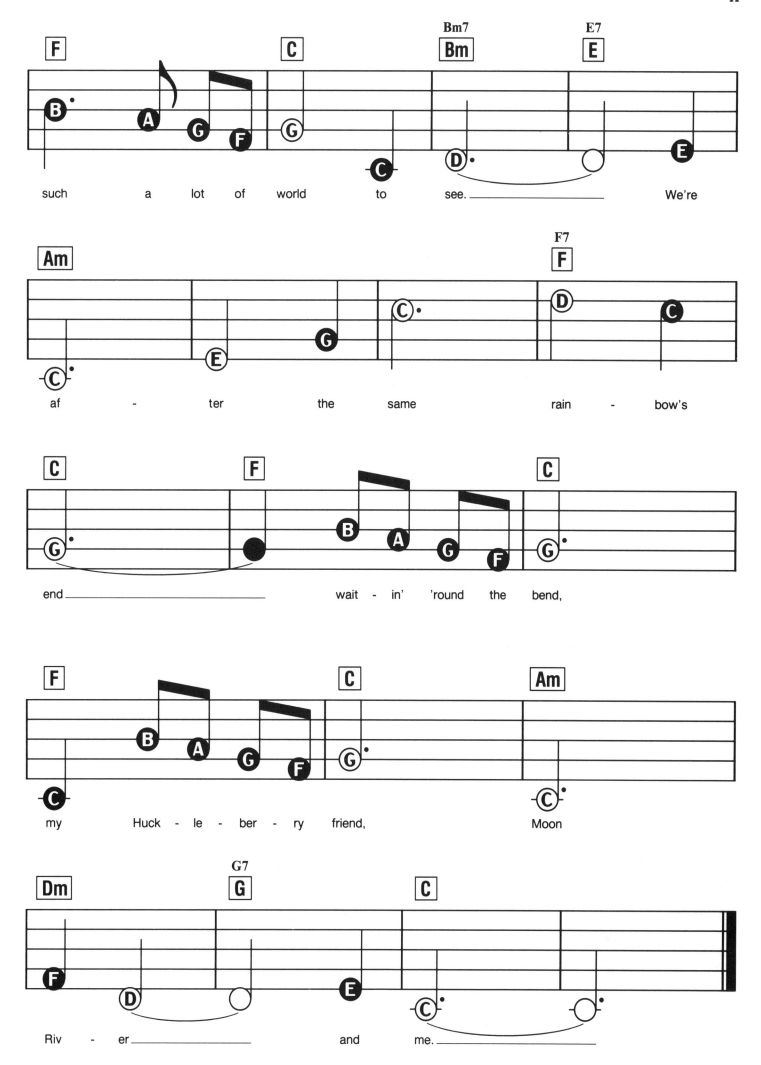

# Nadia's Theme
## from THE YOUNG AND THE RESTLESS

Registration 2
Rhythm: Slow Rock or Ballad

By Barry DeVorzon
and Perry Botkin, Jr.

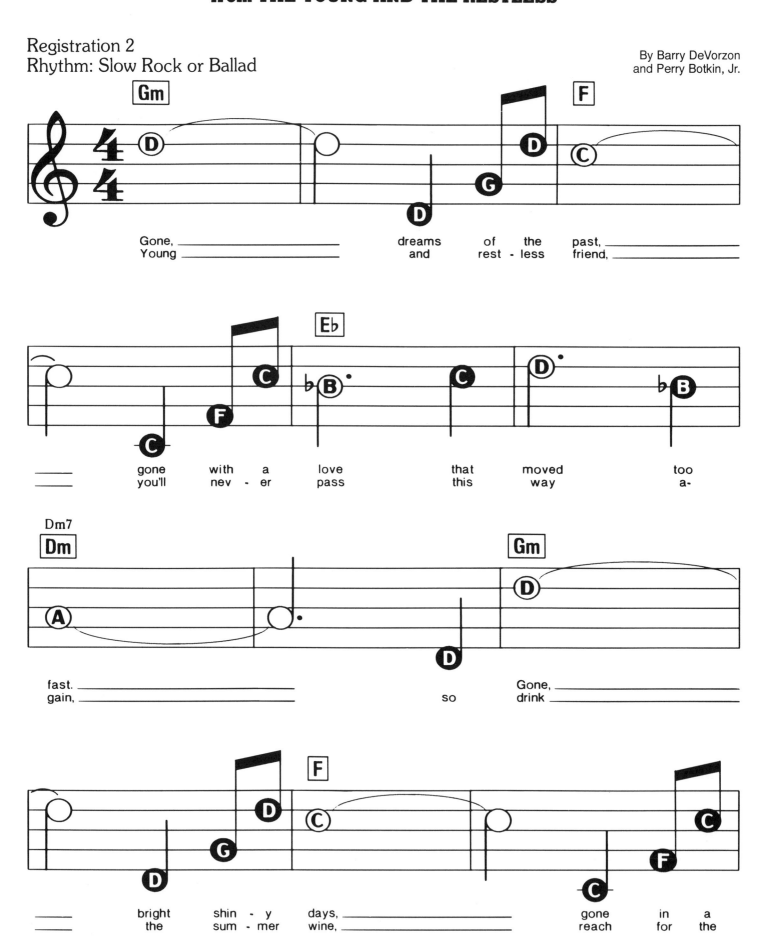

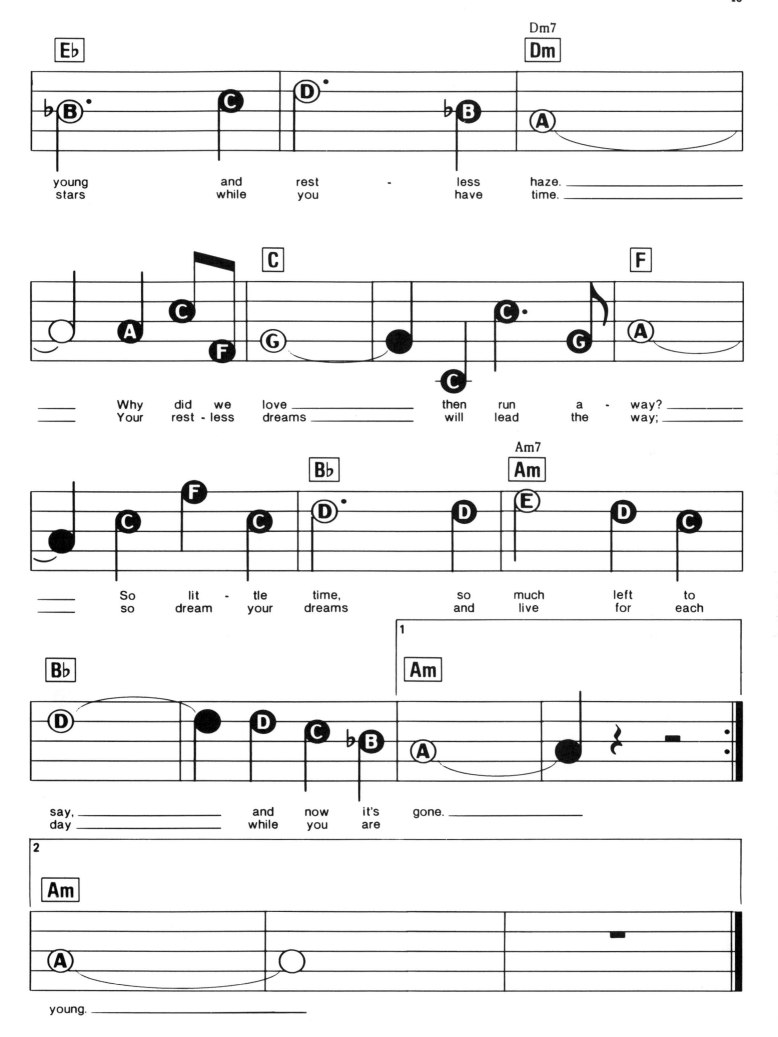

# Raindrops Keep Fallin' on My Head

### from BUTCH CASSIDY AND THE SUNDANCE KID

Registration 5
Rhythm: Swing or Shuffle

Lyric by Hal David
Music by Burt Bacharach

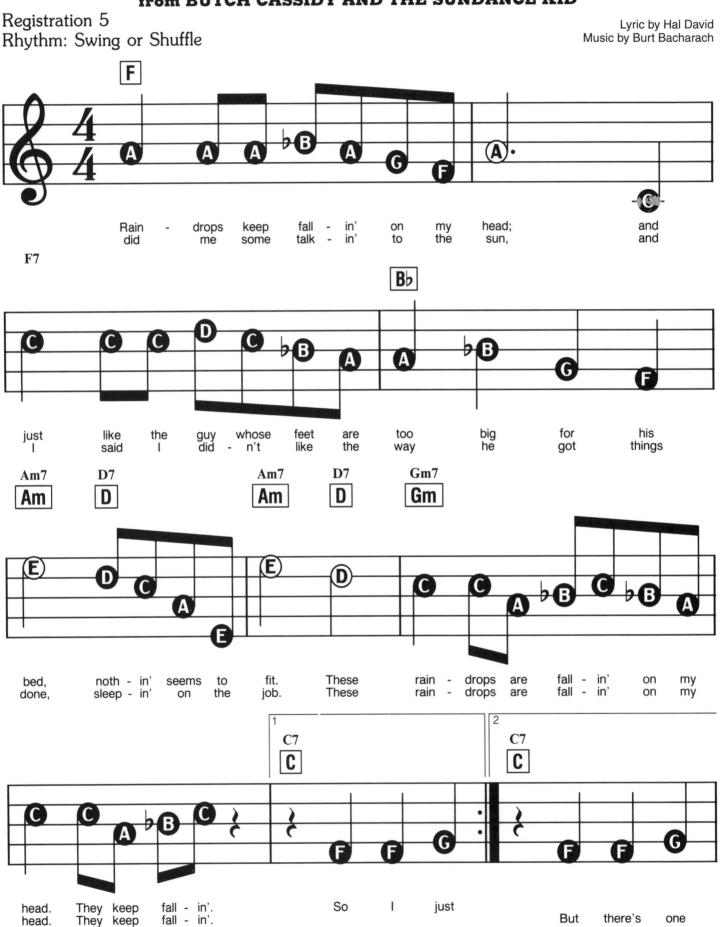

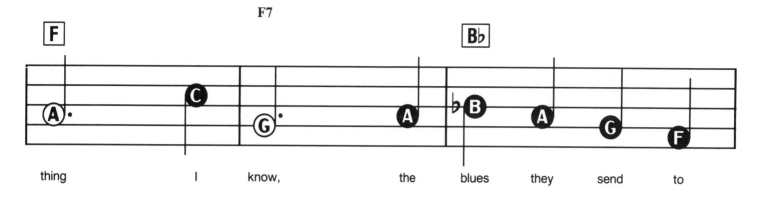

thing I know, the blues they send to

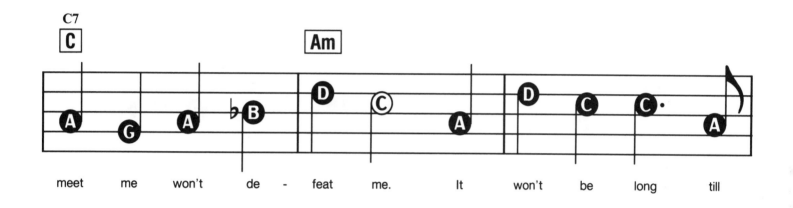

meet me won't de - feat me. It won't be long till

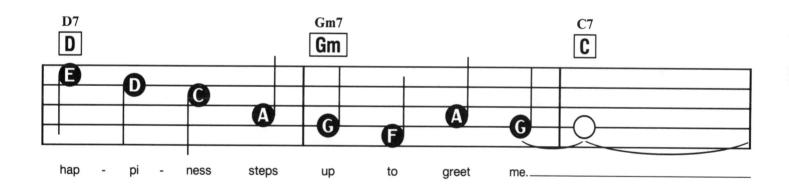

hap - pi - ness steps up to greet me.____

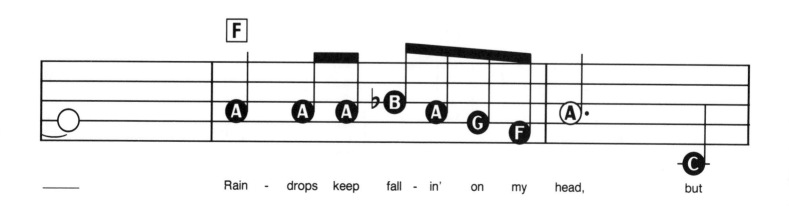

____ Rain - drops keep fall - in' on my head, but

46

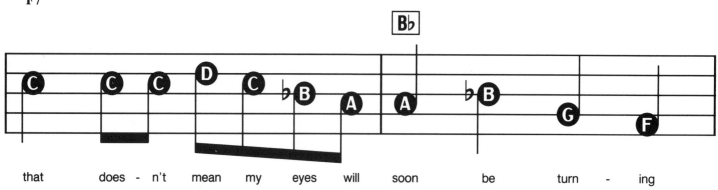

that     does - n't  mean  my  eyes  will   soon    be    turn -    ing

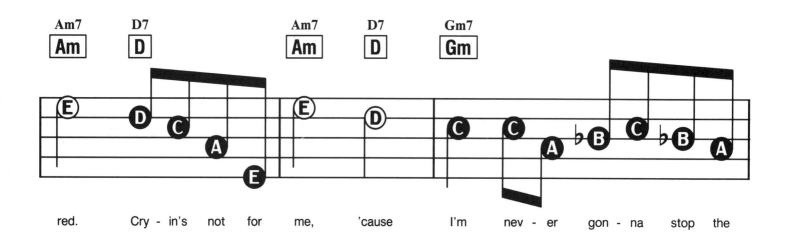

red.   Cry - in's  not  for  me,  'cause   I'm  nev - er   gon - na   stop  the

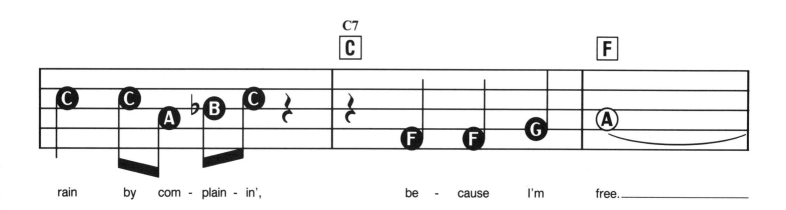

rain   by  com - plain - in',           be - cause  I'm   free._____

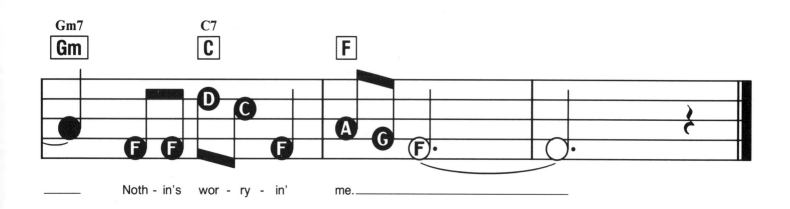

_____  Noth - in's  wor - ry - in'   me._____

# Somewhere Out There
### from AN AMERICAN TAIL

Registration 4
Rhythm: Rock or 8 Beat

Words and Music by James Horner,
Barry Mann and Cynthia Weil

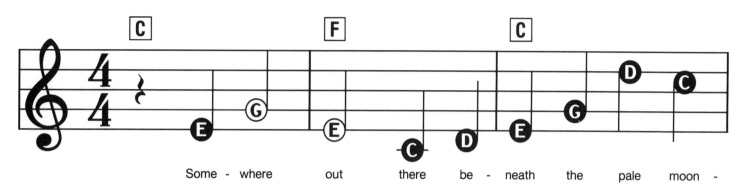

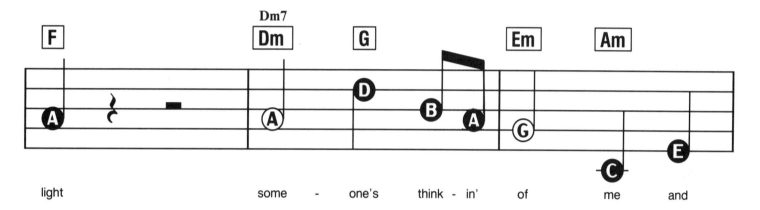

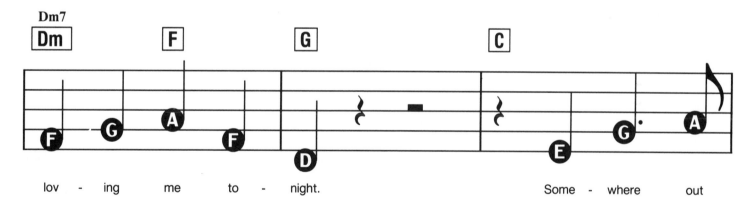

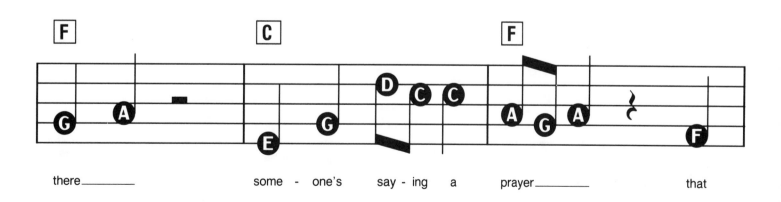

MCA music publishing

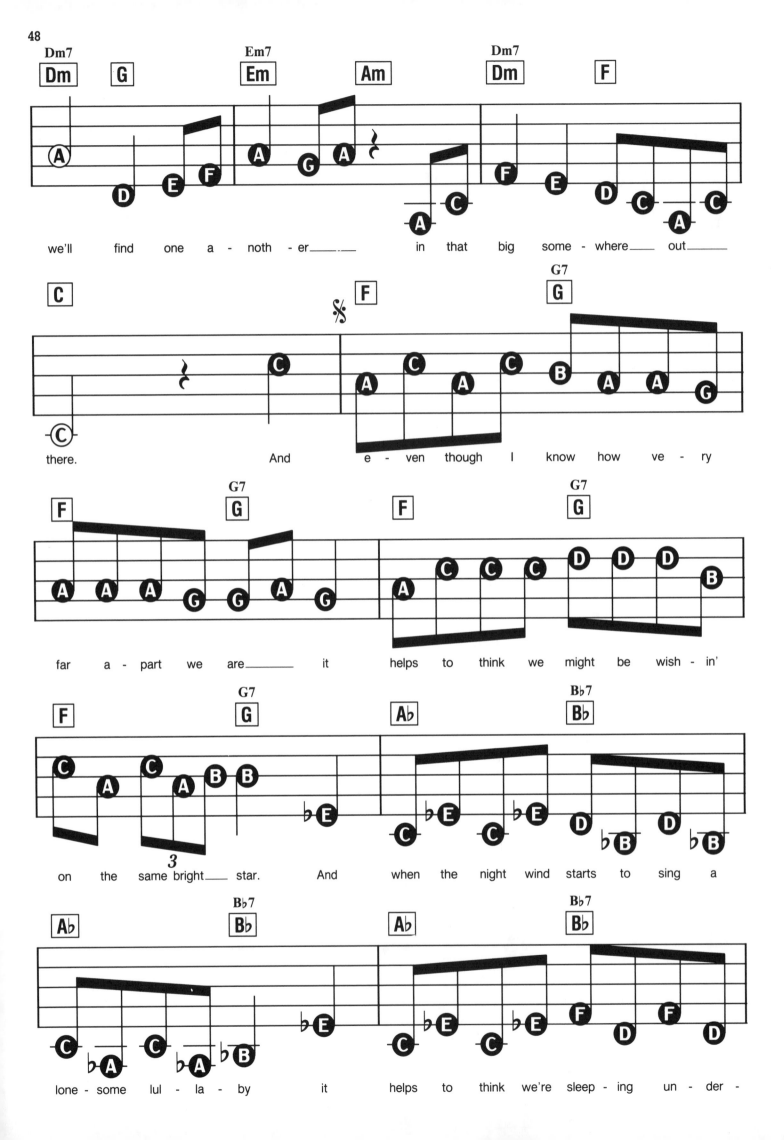

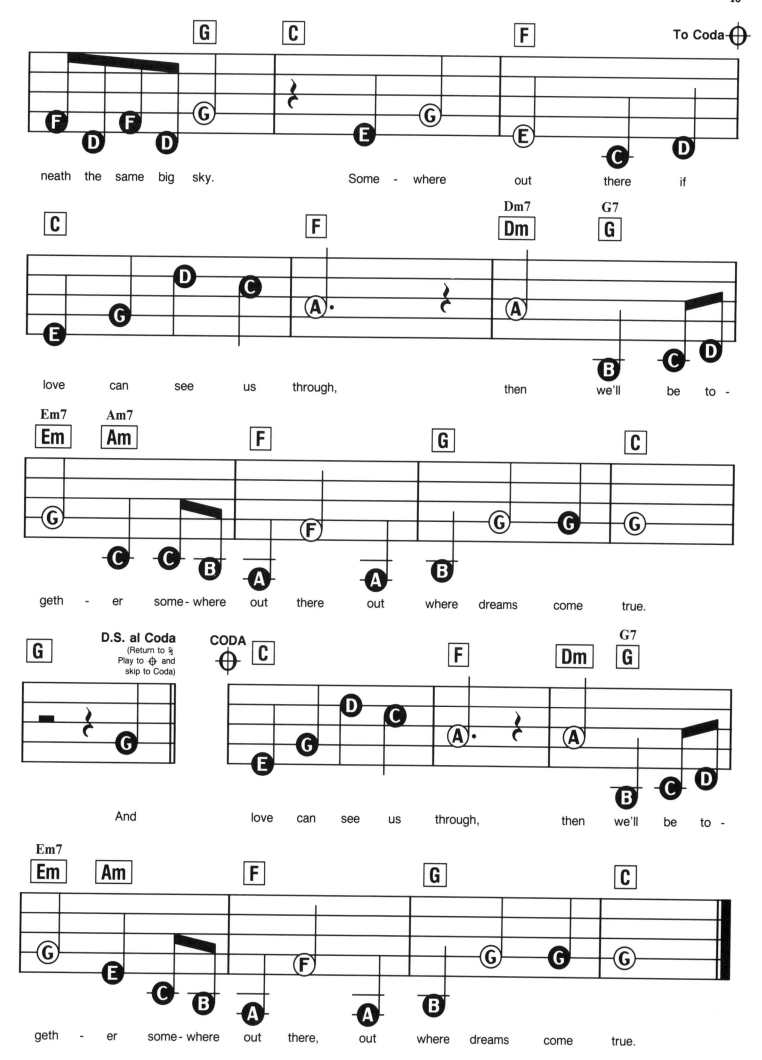

# A Time for Us
## (Love Theme)
### from the Paramount Picture ROMEO AND JULIET

Registration 1
Rhythm: Waltz

Words by Larry Kusik and Eddie Snyder
Music by Nino Rota

51

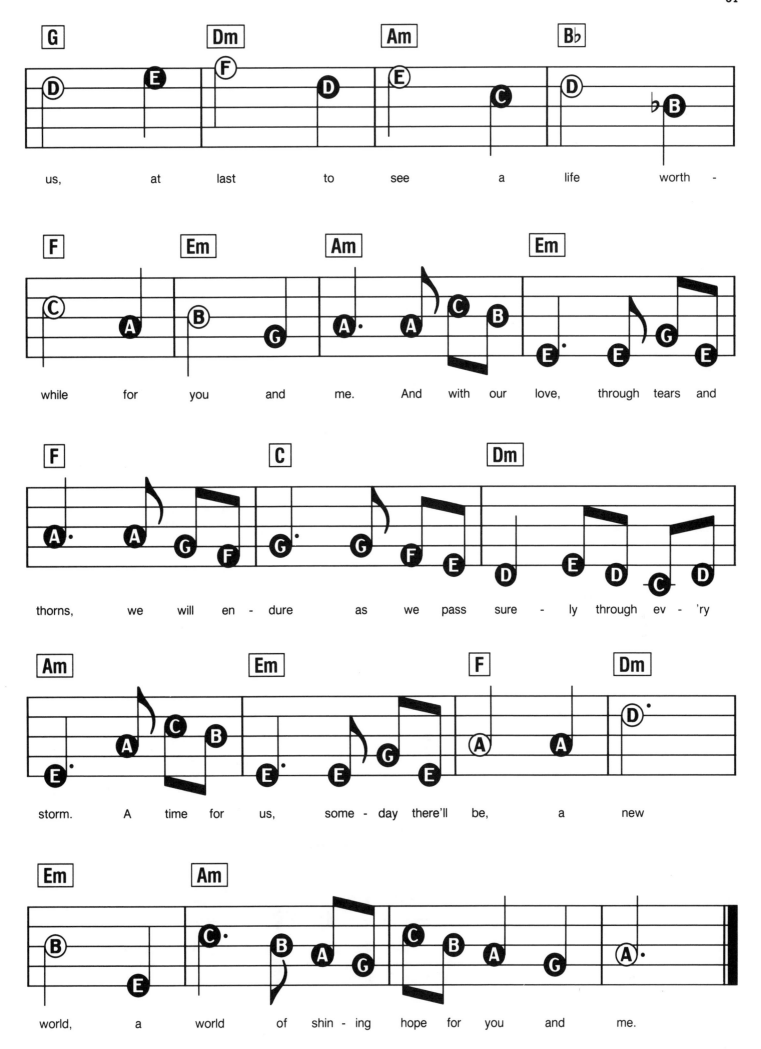

# Vincent
## (Starry Starry Night)

Registration 7
Rhythm: 8 Beat or Pops

Words and Music by
Don McLean

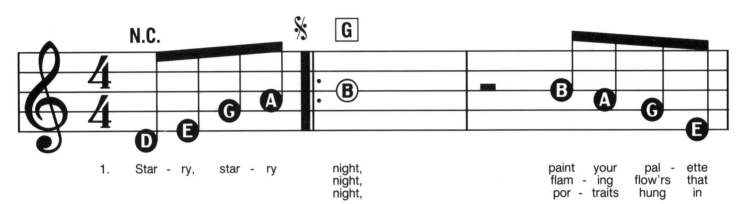

1. Star - ry, star - ry night,
night,
night,

paint your pal - ette
flam - ing flow'rs that
por - traits hung in

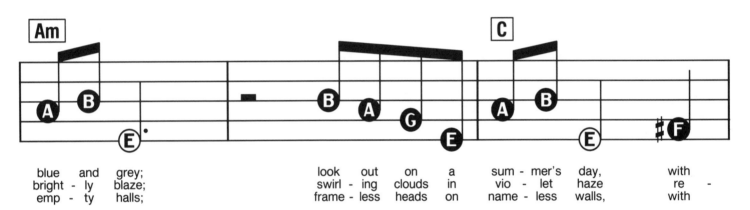

blue and grey;
bright - ly blaze;
emp - ty halls;

look out on a
swirl - ing clouds in
frame - less heads on

sum - mer's day,
vio - let haze
name - less walls,

with
with re -
with

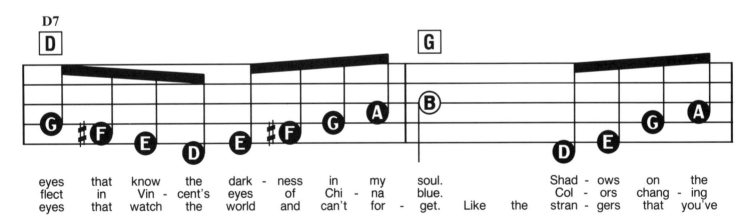

eyes that know the dark - ness in my soul.
flect in Vin - cent's eyes of Chi - na blue.
eyes that watch the world and can't for - get. Like the

Shad - ows on the
Col - ors chang - ing
stran - gers that you've

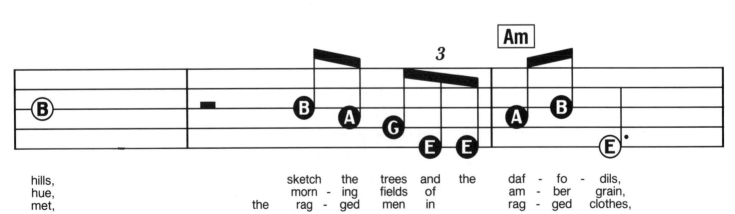

hills,
hue,
met,

sketch the trees and the
morn - ing fields of
the rag - ged men in

daf - fo - dils,
am - ber grain,
rag - ged clothes,

MCA music publishing

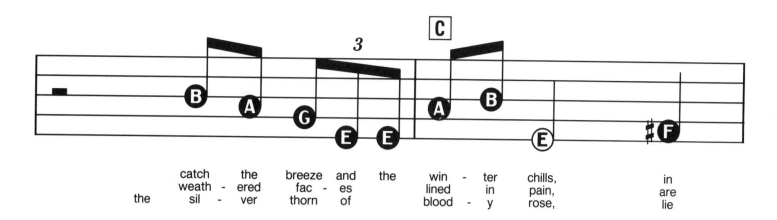

catch   the   breeze  and  the   win - ter   chills,       in
weath - ered   fac - es   the   lined   in   pain,      are
the   sil - ver   thorn  of   blood - y   rose,      lie

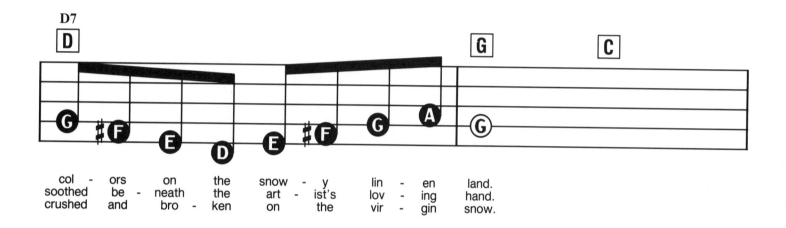

col - ors   on   the   snow - y   lin - en   land.
soothed  be - neath  the  art - ist's  lov - ing  hand.
crushed  and  bro - ken  on  the  vir - gin  snow.

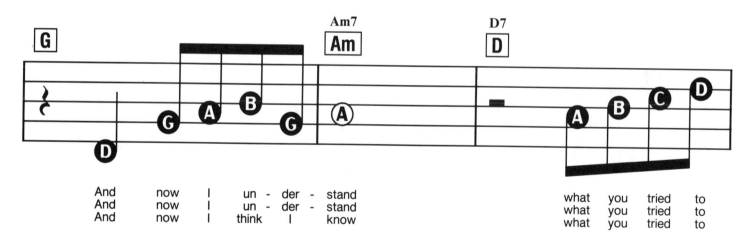

And   now  I  un - der - stand      what  you  tried  to
And   now  I  un - der - stand      what  you  tried  to
And   now  I  think  I  know      what  you  tried  to

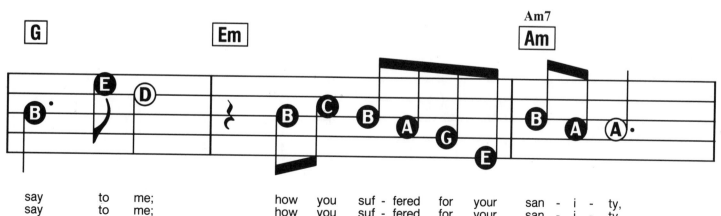

say  to  me;    how  you  suf - fered  for  your  san - i - ty,
say  to  me;    how  you  suf - fered  for  your  san - i - ty,
say  to  me;    how  you  suf - fered  for  your  san - i - ty,

54

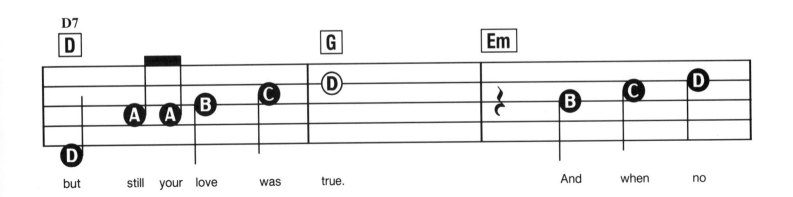

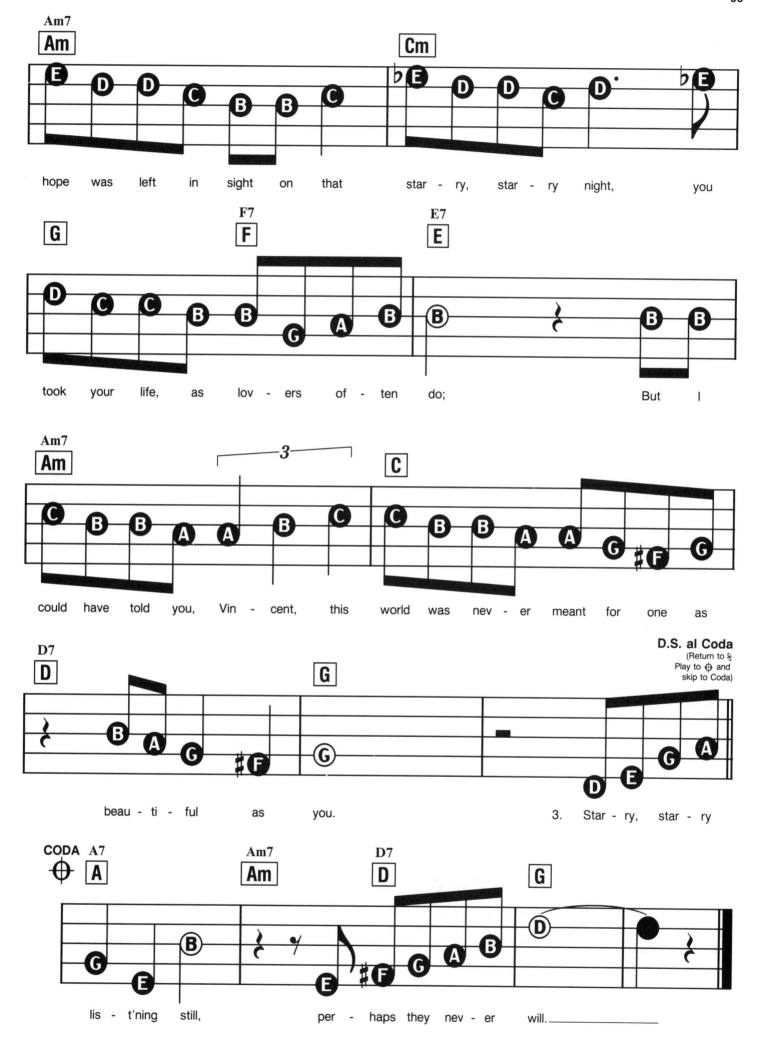

# The Way We Were

Registration 8
Rhythm: Pops or Rock

Words by Alan and Marilyn Bergman
Music by Marvin Hamlisch

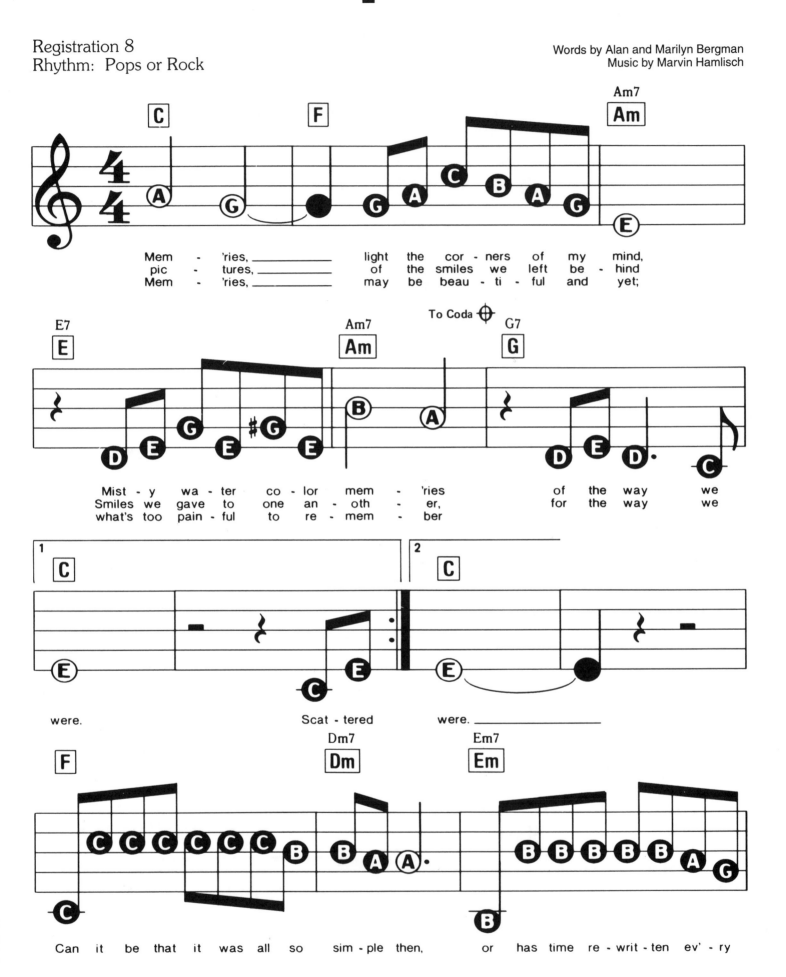

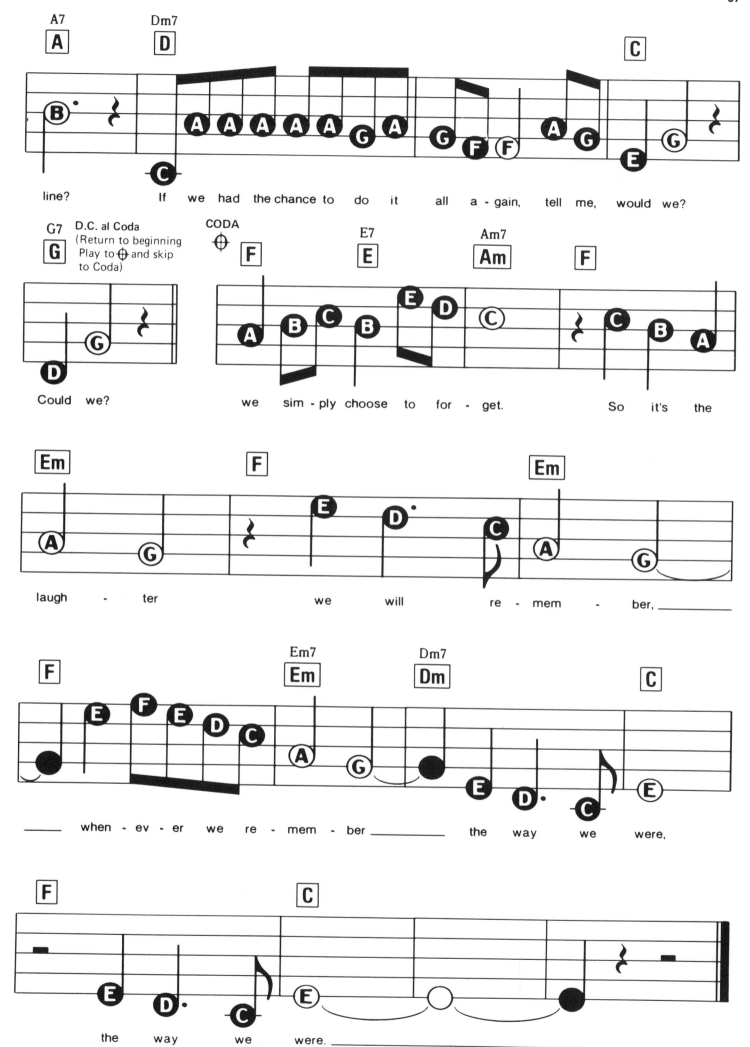

# Where Is Your Heart
## (The Song from MOULIN ROUGE)

Registration 2
Rhythm: Waltz

Words by William Engvick
Music by George Auric

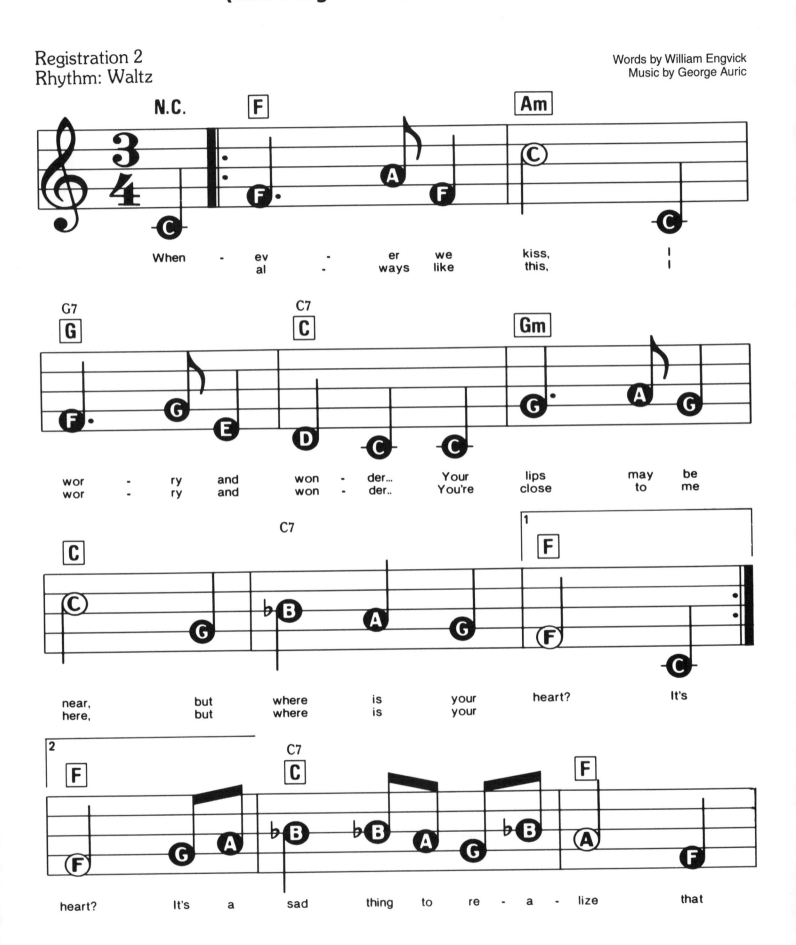

59

# A Swingin' Safari

Registration 8
Rhythm: Fox Trot or Swing

By Bert Kaempfert

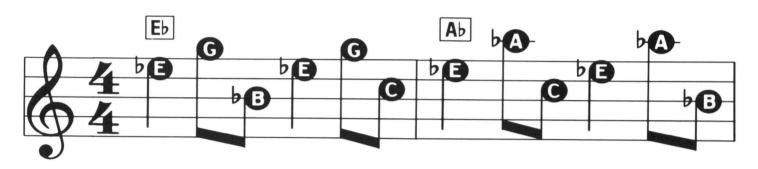

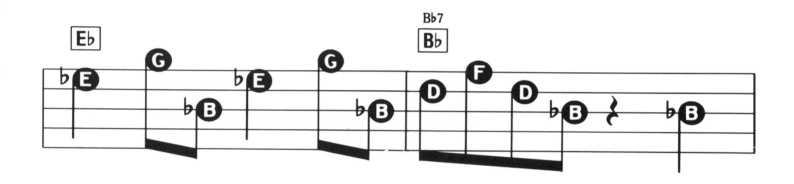

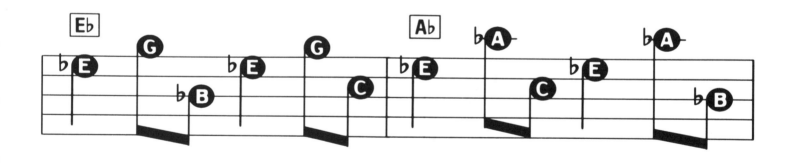

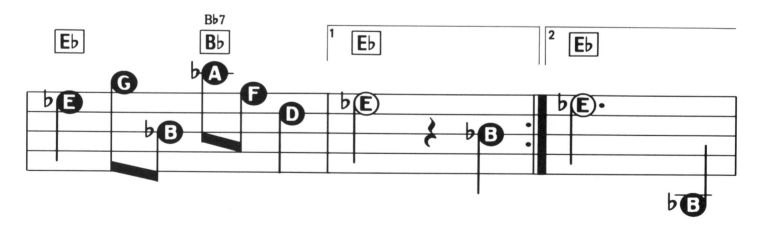

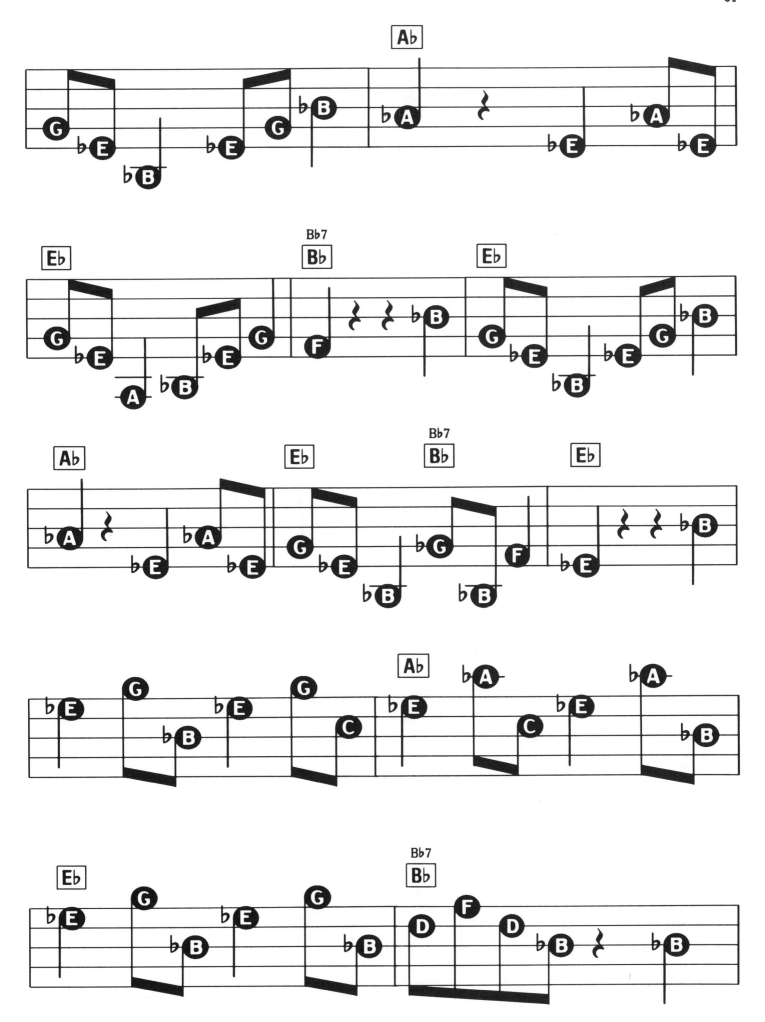

62

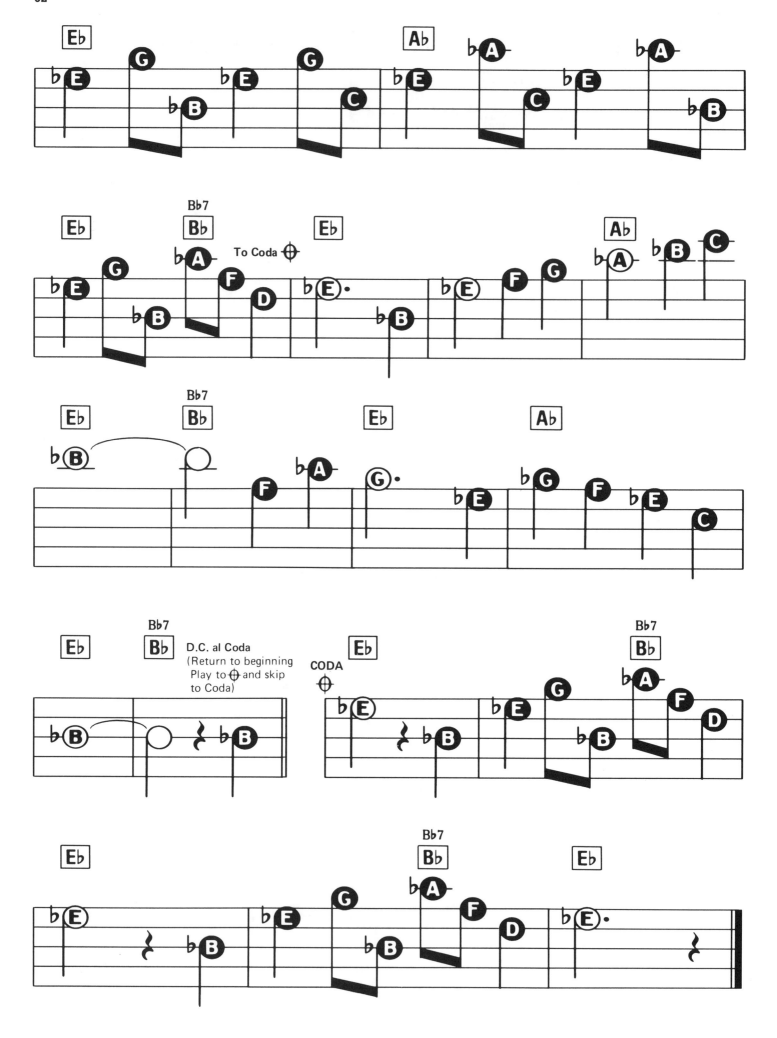

# Registration Guide

- Match the Registration number on the song to the corresponding numbered category below. Select and activate an instrumental sound available on your instrument.

- Choose an automatic rhythm appropriate to the mood and style of the song. (Consult your Owner's Guide for proper operation of automatic rhythm features.)

- Adjust the tempo and volume controls to comfortable settings.

## Registration

| | |
|---|---|
| **1** | Flute, Pan Flute, Jazz Flute |
| **2** | Clarinet, Organ |
| **3** | Violin, Strings |
| **4** | Brass, Trumpet |
| **5** | Synth Ensemble, Accordion, Brass |
| **6** | Pipe Organ, Harpsichord |
| **7** | Jazz Organ, Vibraphone, Vibes, Electric Piano, Jazz Guitar |
| **8** | Piano, Electric Piano |
| **9** | Trumpet, Trombone, Clarinet, Saxophone, Oboe |
| **10** | Violin, Cello, Strings |